The Plain Truth About

THE PROTESTANT REFORMATION

By Roderick C. Meredith

*More than 500 years ago, the Protestant Reformation
completely transformed the religious world. But was
it a return to the "faith once delivered"? Or was it
something else entirely? You need to know the truth!*

PR Edition 1.0 | March 2019
©2019 Living Church of God™
All rights reserved. Printed in the U.S.A.

ISBN: 978-1-62479-997-6

Contents

Chapter I

The Plain Truth About the Protestant Reformation

The Protestant movement today is on trial. The Protestant Reformation has spawned a veritable Babylon of hundreds of differing denominations. They vary in faith and practice all the way from fundamentalist Quakers to modern Congregationalists, from primitive Methodists to Christian Scientists, from conservative Lutherans to Mormons, Seventh-Day Adventists and Jehovah's Witnesses—with hundreds of shadings in between.

What is the real basis of the Protestant churches throughout the world today? Why did their early leaders revolt against the authority of the Roman Catholic Church? To what extent are they responsible for today's "divided Christendom"?

Did the Protestant reformers succeed in attaining their stated goals? More importantly, did they succeed in recapturing the faith and belief of Jesus and the inspired New Testament Church? For the real question is whether the Protestant reformers and their successors have succeeded in returning to the "faith which was once for all delivered" (Jude 3).

These questions are *vital*. Many of us have been reared from childhood in one of the many denominations or sects stemming from the Protestant Reformation. We assumed—as *every* child does—that what we were taught was altogether true.

Of course, we were, however, all taught *different* things!

We are told in Scripture to *"Prove* all things; hold fast that which is good" (1 Thessalonians 5:21, *King James Version*). The purpose of this work, then, is an objective examination of the real factors underlying the Protestant Reformation. We will seek to find out *why* the early reformers rebelled against the Roman Catholic system, and *why* the various Protestant bodies took shape as they did. Using the impartial facts of history, we will compare, in principle, the *teachings*, *methods* and *actions* of the Protestant reformers with the Bible, which they professed to follow.

The Basis of Judgment

Realizing the current trend toward modernism and rejection of the Bible as an inspired authority, let us simply state that this work is written from the point of view of a fundamentalist, literal understanding of the Bible. This inspired revelation from God will provide the criteria of truth.

For those readers who may be modernists, or "higher critics," we will simply ask: Have you really *proved* whether or not the Bible is supernaturally inspired? A good way to disprove it would be to present conclusive evidence that the scores of prophecies, which pronounce specific judgments on the major cities and nations of the ancient world, have not come to pass. Unfortunately for your cause, no one has been able to do this.

Another test would be to take God at His word, surrender to obey His will, and then in real faith and earnest, believing prayer, claim one of the many specific promises given in the Bible and *see* whether or not a miracle-working God stands behind His word.

Naturally, the modernist has not done that. He has *failed* to prove that the Bible is not inspired. So, it may be well to remind ourselves that it is intellectual hypocrisy to scoff and ridicule something when there is *no proof* to the contrary.

Therefore, we will employ the Holy Bible as the overall spiritual "yardstick" against which we will measure the Protestant Reformation.

Also, we shall quote the statements of the reformers themselves about what they intended to do. We will examine the historical record to see what they actually did do. Then we will consider statements of their Protestant descendants, and let *them* help pass judgment on the ultimate results of the Reformation.

The Protestant Aims

We will examine the well-known saying of William Chillingworth, the Protestant theologian: "The Bible, the whole Bible, and nothing but the Bible, is the religion of Protestants" (Schaff-Herzog 3: 29). In their constant affirmation of the Scriptures as "the inspired rule of faith and practice" (Schaff 1: 257), the Protestant leaders have committed themselves to follow the religion of Jesus Christ and His Apostles in all respects.

The Lutherans, in their *Torgau Book* of 1576, declare that "the *only standard* by which all dogmas and all teachers must be valued and judged is no other than the prophetic and Apostolic writings of the Old and of the New Testaments" (Lindsay 467).

The average Protestant of today usually accepts these statements at face value and assumes that they must be at least very close to the truth. We would ask: Was this actually true during the course of the Protestant Reformation? Is it true now?

It is well to remember also that in his writings and teachings, John Knox, among other leading reformers, acknowledged "that all worshipping, honouring, or service of God invented by the brain of man in the religion of God without His own express commandment is idolatry." He then adds force and pointedness to his statement by saying that "it shall nothing excuse you to say, we trust not in idols, for so will every idolater allege; but if either you or they in God's honour do anything contrary to God's Word, you show yourself to put your trust in somewhat else besides God, and so are idolaters. Mark, brethren, that many maketh an idol of their own wisdom or phantasy; more trusting to that which they think good not unto God" (Hastie 50).

Knox's warning against false "service of God invented by the brain of man" is certainly parallel to Jesus' condemnation of the "traditions of men" (Mark 7:7–8). It is very important that we understand this principle before attempting to comprehend the real meaning of the Protestant Reformation, for, as Solomon wisely wrote: "There is a way that seems right to a man, but its end is the way of death" (Proverbs 14:12).

We must not view the Reformation in the light of human ideas and what appears reasonable to man, but in the light of Christ's words: "Man shall not live by bread alone, but by every word of God" (Luke 4:4). We need to consider also Jesus' warning against human tradition, and the fact that the reformers understood this principle and claimed to pursue a course based upon the Bible alone.

Was God's True Church "Reformed"?

Although it is a subject many Protestants do not like to discuss, to correctly grasp the significance of the Reformation, we must take one other very important consideration into account. That is, was the Protestant movement a reformation of God's true Church gone wrong? Is, then, the Roman Catholic Church actually the misguided offspring of the Church Jesus Christ said He would build?

If not, was the Protestant movement simply an effort of men to extricate themselves from a false and harsh system, which they admit is pagan and devilish in many of its beliefs and practices? In that case, *where had God's true Church been* in all the centuries between the original Apostles and the Protestant reformers?

Jesus Christ said: "I will build *My church*; and the gates of Hades shall not prevail against it" (Matthew 16:18). At the conclusion of His earthly ministry, He commanded His Apostles: "Go therefore and make disciples of all the nations, baptizing them in the name of the Father and of the Son and of the Holy Spirit, *teaching them to observe all things that I have commanded* you; and lo, I *am with you always,* even to the end of the age" (Matthew 28:19–20).

At the start of the Reformation, where was the Church Jesus built, the Church to which He promised, "I am with you always"? If it was the Roman Catholic Church, then the Protestants were simply—as Catholic historians claim—revolting against the Church of God on earth.

In this case, much as they might wish to improve conditions *within* the true church, they should have remembered and obeyed the words Christ uttered of the Scribes and Pharisees—the perverse, but rightfully constituted religious leaders of His day: "Therefore whatever they tell you to observe, that observe and do, but do not do according to their works..." (Matthew 23:3).

But, if it is the case that the church of Rome is not the Church that Jesus built, then *why did not the reformers seek for and unite with that Church which had never participated in the paganism of Rome,* nor been contaminated by her false doctrine and influence, the Church which Jesus promised to be with until the end of the age, the Church of which He is the living Head (Ephesians 1:22)?

Why start *many new churches* if that *one true Church* was still in existence?

Or was it necessary only to purify the faith and morals of those *individuals* who would be willing to come out of a corrupted Roman system?

These questions *demand* an answer! As we shall later see, many Protestant leaders—knowing and believing that Rome is their true source—seek to vindicate her claim as the true body of Christ on earth. This supposition needs a careful examination.

Is the "mother" church at Rome the only historical basis of the Protestant plea of descent from Christ and His apostles? We shall see.

Today's "Christendom"

We must weigh any religious denomination or movement in the balance of Christ's prophetic saying: "You will know them by their fruits. Do men gather grapes from thornbushes or figs from thistles? Even so, every good tree bears good fruit, but a bad tree bears bad fruit" (Matthew 7:16–17).

The honest historian will be forced to admit that the Reformation brought in its wake an increased interest in, and knowledge of, the Bible by the common man. Also, the revival of learning and the arts inspired by the Renaissance spread most readily to the whole populace of those nations which accepted Protestantism. Admittedly, the Protestant lands maintain a far higher level of education than do Catholic nations. And, in like manner, they enjoy a much higher standard of living, materially speaking.

But, again returning to the real root of the problem, how do the *spiritual* standards of modern Protestants compare with that of the inspired New Testament Church?

Has a real return to the original Christianity of the Apostles occurred? Or does, of necessity, another tremendous "cleansing and purging" religious upheaval still lie in the future?

Speaking to His disciples about the Pharisees, the religious leaders of His day, Christ said: "Every plant which My heavenly Father has not planted will be uprooted" (Matthew 15:13). Are the "fruits," the *results*, of the Protestant Reformation such as to show us that this movement was planted by God and used for His glory?

The purpose of this book is to answer these vital questions and to get at the very root of them.

Let us be reminded again, at the outset, that the Protestant Reformation must be viewed by every honest Christian in the light of the clear teachings and examples of Christ and the Apostles—"the Bible, the whole Bible, and nothing but the Bible," which Protestant leaders have claimed to be their sole "rule of faith and practice."

If the Protestant faith be true, then we can *prove* that it is so. But we must not *assume*, without proof, that the doctrines, beliefs, and practices of modern Protestantism constitute the religion founded by Jesus Christ, the Son of God.

In this, above all other matters, we must *know*. We must be *sure*. We must not be afraid to compare Christ and His word with what purports to be His Church in our age.

This is a fair challenge.

Christianity after the Death of the Apostles

All scholars agree that the Protestant reformers broke with the historical Catholic Church. Very few laymen, however, realize the history of degeneracy and the utter depravity to which that body had sunk before the call to reform was sounded. A realization of this fact, and a grasp of the historical background of the Protestant Reformation, is most necessary for its proper understanding.

It is widely recognized that the *visible* church in the early Roman Empire *completely changed* many of the beliefs and practices of Christ and the Apostles. We need to understand the nature of these changes to properly evaluate the later Reformation. And as we consider the record of the Roman system, we should ask ourselves: "Is this the history of God's true Church gone wrong?"

Early Apostasy

A mysterious change transformed the life, doctrine, and worship of the visible Church within fifty years after the death of the original Apostles. As Jesse Lyman Hurlbut observes: "For fifty years after St. Paul's life a curtain hangs over the church, through which we strive vainly to look; and when at last it rises, about 120AD, with the writings of the earliest church-fathers, we find a church *in many aspects very different* from that in the days of St. Peter and St. Paul" (Hurlbut, *The Story of the Christian Church* 41).

This unusual transformation recalls the ominous words of Paul: "For the time will come when they will not endure sound doctrine, but according to their own desires, because they have itching ears, they will heap up for themselves teachers; and they will turn their ears away from the truth, and be turned aside to fables" (2 Timothy 4:3–4). Peter, in his second epistle, had given a similar warning: "But there were also false prophets among the people, even as there will be false teachers among you, who will secretly bring in destructive heresies, even denying the Lord who bought them, and bring on themselves swift destruction. And many will follow their destructive ways, because of whom the way of truth will be blasphemed" (2 Peter 2:1–2).

In fact, by the time of the Apostle John's last epistle, about 90AD, perversions of the true faith were already rampant, and false teachers were gaining the ascendancy within the visible Church congregations. John states that one Diotrephes was already excommunicating those who adhere to the truth, and "not content with that, he himself does not receive the brethren, and forbids those who wish to, putting them out of the church" (3 John 9–10).

From the detached viewpoint of the secular historian, Edward Gibbon describes this portion of Church history: "A more melancholy duty is imposed on the historian. He must discover the inevitable mixture of *error* and *corruption* which she contracted in a long residence upon earth, among a weak and degenerate race of beings" (Gibbon 1: 380).

The visible Christian assemblies, subverted by false teachers with worldly ambitions, began to adopt the practices and customs of the ancient pagans in place of the inspired faith and practice of the apostolic Church. "Christianity began already to wear the garb of heathenism" (Wharey 39).

Ceremonies and rituals began to replace the worship of God from the heart until finally the whole of religion was made to consist of little else (Wharey 40). This, of course, was true only of the *visible* church as a whole.

Some Continue Apostolic Practice

In spite of the apostasy of the majority, there is an abundance of historical evidence to indicate that a number of Christian societies—some holding much of the truth, some very little—continued to follow the basic doctrines and practices of the original Church right down to the time of the Reformation. Gibbon speaks of the plight of the principal imitators of the Apostolic Church, called the

"Nazarenes," who *"had laid the foundations* of the Church (but) soon found themselves overwhelmed by the increasing multitudes, that from all the various religions of Polytheism enlisted under the banner of Christ: and the Gentiles, who, with the approbation of their peculiar apostle, had rejected the intolerable weight of the Mosaic ceremonies, at length refused to their more scrupulous brethren the same toleration which at first they had humbly solicited for their own practice" (Gibbon 387).

Thus, we find that the Gentile converts began bringing into the Church the customs of their former heathen religions, and an *attitude of contempt* for those who would remain faithful to the example and practice of Christ and the original Apostles. No doubt this very attitude was the reason Diotrephes could "cast out" the true brethren with the apparent approval of the visible congregations.

Since it is not the purpose of this treatise to trace the history of the small body of believers who remained faithful to the original Church's faith and worship, and since it is a common practice for denominational church historians to distort or cast aspersions upon the belief of this people, it may be well to include an admission by Hurlbut of the difficulty in ascertaining the true beliefs of these people, or, for that matter, of the actual "heresies" of the time. He tells us:

> With regard to these sects and so-called heresies, one difficulty in understanding them arises from the fact that (except with the Montanists, and even there in large measure) their own writings have perished; and we are dependent for our views upon those who wrote against them, and were undoubtedly prejudiced. Suppose, for example, that the Methodists, as a denomination, had passed out of existence with all their literature; and a thousand years afterward, scholars should attempt to ascertain their teachings out of the books and pamphlets written *against* John Wesley in the eighteenth century, what wrong conclusions would be reached, and what a distorted portrait of Methodism would be presented! (Hurlbut 66).

Add to this scanty historical evidence, the fact that many modern church historians write from a denominational viewpoint prejudicial to Apostolic practices and beliefs, and it is easy to perceive the inherent difficulty in finding the truth about such Christians in past ages. Nevertheless, even the testimony of enemies contains abundant proof that an unbroken chain of these faithful believers has existed until this day.

The Development of the Catholic Church

Although, as we have seen, much of the truth perished from the local congregations within fifty years after the death of the Apostles, the Roman Catholic Church as such did not develop until the fourth century. Before then, there were many splits and divisions within the visible church, but the progress of literal idolatry was stayed because of persecution by the Roman state—which prevented many of the heathen from coming in and kept the Church pure to that extent.

But, even so, it was mainly a purity in *error*, for the theology of the time had departed so far from the teachings of Jesus and the Apostles that many doctrines were now based upon the ideas of Plato and other pagan philosophers. Origen, one of the great "church fathers" of this period, was an admirer of this philosophy and employed it in explaining the doctrines of the gospel. This led him to the *allegorical method* of interpreting the Holy Scripture (Wharey 46).

Dealing with this period, Gibbon describes for us the gradual development of what eventually became the Roman Catholic hierarchy, patterned after the government of imperial Rome. He states: "The primitive Christians were dead to the business and pleasures of the world; but their love of action, which could never be entirely extinguished, soon revived, and found a new occupation in the government of the church" (Gibbon 410).

Of the development of this church government, he tells us that it soon followed the model of the provincial synods—uniting several churches in one area under the leadership of the bishop of the church possessing the most members and usually situated in the largest city (Gibbon 413–415). With the conversion of Constantine to nominal Christianity, the church government began to be modeled more nearly after the Roman state. Wharey tells us: "Under Constantine the Great, the church first became connected with the state, and in its *government* was accommodated to such connection, upon principles of state policy" (Wharey 55).

Corruption and Moral Decay

The increased vice and corruption of the ministry is related by John Mosheim, who aptly describes the *lust for power* that entered the hearts and minds of the spiritual leaders of this period:

> The bishops had *shameful quarrels* among themselves, respecting the boundaries of their sees and the extent of their jurisdiction; and while they trampled on the rights of the people and of the inferior clergy, they vied with the civil governors of the provinces in luxury, arrogance, and voluptuousness (Mosheim 131).

When Constantine became sole emperor of the Roman Empire in 323AD, within a year Christianity, at least in name, was recognized as the official religion of the empire. This recognition not only affected the government of the church and the morals of its ministers, but it had a profound influence on the entire church and its membership.

All persecution of the established church ceased at once and forever. The ancient "day of the sun" was soon proclaimed as a day of rest and worship. Heathen temples were consecrated as churches. Ministers soon became a privileged class, above the law of the land.

Now everybody sought membership in the church. "Ambitious, worldly, unscrupulous men sought office in the church for social and political influence" (Hurlbut 79). Instead of Christianity influencing and transforming the world, we see the world dominating the professing Christian church.

> The services of worship increased in splendor, but were less spiritual and hearty than those of former times. The forms and ceremonies of *paganism* gradually crept into the worship. Some of the old *heathen feasts* became church festivals with change of name and worship. About 405 A.D., *images* of saints and martyrs began to appear in the churches... (Hurlbut 79).

The church and state became *one integrated system* when Christianity was adopted as the religion of the empire. The Roman Catholic system had begun, and Hurlbut tells us that "the church gradually usurped power over the state, and the result was not *Christianity*, but a more or less corrupt *hierarchy* controlling the nations of Europe making the church mainly a political machine" (Hurlbut 80).

Catholicism in Power

Within two years after what was called Christianity became the official religion of the Roman Empire, a new capital was chosen and built by Constantine. He selected the Greek city of Byzantium because its situation rendered it relatively safe from the ravages of war which had so often plagued Rome.

Soon after this, the division of the empire took place—with Constantine appointing associate emperors for the West. The division of the empire prepared the way for the coming split in the Catholic Church. This also provided an easier path to the exaltation of the Roman bishop, as he was not now overshadowed by the emperor.

During this time, the established church ruled supreme—and any attempt to return to the Apostolic faith would have been severely punished as an offense against the state. "The command was issued that no one should write or speak against the Christian (Catholic) religion, and all books of its opposers should be burned" (Hurlbut 85).

Thus, we can see that those who may have held much truth during this period were deprived of the means of preserving any record of their faith for future generations. This edict was effective in stamping out *heresy*, but it was also effective in stifling any *truth* that was held in opposition to Catholic doctrine.

As for the substance of that doctrine, Wharey tells us:

> The *Theology* of this century began to be much adulterated and corrupted with superstition and heathen philosophy. Hence, are to be seen evident traces of excessive veneration for departed saints, of a belief in a state of *purgatory* for souls after death, of the celibacy of the clergy, of the *worship of images* and *relics*, and of many other opinions, which in process of time almost banished the true religion or at least very much obscured and corrupted it (Wharey 60).

Thus, we find that as the Catholic Church continued, superstition, heathenism, and idolatry increased.

The development of papal power was the outstanding fact during the ten centuries of the Middle Ages. The Pope at Rome soon claimed to be ruler, not only over the other bishops, but over *nations, kings,* and *emperors* (Hurlbut 105).

Gregory I (590–604) made the church the virtual ruler in the province around Rome, and it was he who developed the doctrine of purgatory, the adoration of images, and transubstantiation. George Park Fisher speaks of this period: "*Christmas* originated in the West (Rome), and from there passed over into the Eastern Church. Many Christians still took part in the *heathen* festival of *New Year's*" (Fisher, *The History of the Christian Church* 119).

Speaking of the doctrinal controversies that raged through the church at this time, he says: "The interference of the state in matters of doctrine is a fact that calls for particular notice. In philosophy, Plato's influence was still predominant: Augustine as well as Origen, was steeped in the Platonic spirit" (Fisher, *The History of the Christian Church* 121). Here is a plain statement that the philosophical teachings of such heathen thinkers as Plato distinctly influenced the doctrinal positions of many of the early "church fathers"!

The Culmination and Decline of Papal Prestige

The height of papal supremacy was attained under Gregory VII, born Hildebrand. Under his reign, we behold the spectacle of the current emperor, Henry IV, in order to receive absolution from the pope's ban of excommunication, "having laid aside all belongings of royalty, with bare feet and clad in wool, continued for three days to stand before the gates of the castle" (Hurlbut 111).

Another high point in the progress of papal authority was the reign of Innocent III. He declared in his inaugural discourse, "The successor of St. Peter stands midway between God and man; below God, above man; Judge of all, judged of none" (Hurlbut 112).

Soon after this, however, followed the period known as the "Babylonish Captivity" of the church (1305–1378). Through political influence of the French king, the papacy was transferred from Rome to the south of France at Avignon. The political and moral scandals of the pope and clergy throughout this entire period weakened the papal influence, and began to prepare men's minds for the later attempts at reformation (Mosheim 490).

That there were many good and sincere men in the Roman Church even during this period is not doubted. But the *complete departure* of their ancestors from the doctrine and practice of Christ and the Apostles, the substitution in their place of *heathen* philosophies and doctrines of *heathen* church festivals, fasts, images, relics, and sundry other practices—all this would have made it virtually impossible for most men to grasp the simple truths of the Bible, even if they had desired to do so. And, due to the prevailing ignorance and barbarism of the times, most of the common men and women would have been unable to read the Scriptures even if they had been made available, and they had wished to do so (Mosheim 491).

Nevertheless, the constant abuse of ecclesiastical authority by an ignorant and ravenous clergy, the continuing scandals of the papal court, and the compromising involvement of the popes and cardinals in temporal as well as religious affairs—all these things did much to arouse a questioning spirit in the masses of people.

At the conclusion of the "Babylonish Captivity" in 1378, Pope Gregory XI returned to Rome. But at his death, through political pressure and maneuver, *two* popes were elected by the cardinals! The world then beheld the spectacle of the nominal heads of Christendom hurling maledictions, threats, accusations, and excommunications at each other over a period of many years.

Mosheim aptly describes this unhappy state of affairs:

> For, during fifty years the church had two or three heads, and the contemporary pontiffs assailed each other with excommunications, maledictions, and plots. The calamities and distress of those times are indescribable. For besides the perpetual contentions and wars between the pontifical factions, which were ruinous to great numbers, involving them in the loss of life or of property, nearly all sense of religion was in many places extinguished, and wickedness daily acquired greater impunity and boldness; the clergy, previously corrupt, now laid aside even the appearance of piety and godliness, while those who called themselves Christ's vicegerents were at open war with each other and the conscientious people, who believed no one could be saved without living in subjection to Christ's vicar, were thrown into the greatest perplexity and anxiety of mind (Mosheim 496).

Such was the provocative state of "Christendom" on the eve of the Reformation. Well might men have asked themselves, "Is *this* the Church that Jesus Christ built?"

Precursors of the Reformation

History seems to provide some strange dilemmas. One of two alternatives is often assumed about the existence of the true Church during the Middle ages. One is that the Church of God as a visible, organized body of believers had ceased to exist over a period embracing hundreds of years. The other is that the Roman Catholic Church—whose *utter depravity* we have described—was the only legitimate descendant of the Church Jesus Christ said He would build (Matthew 16:18).

However, many historians are now beginning to realize that there were groups of believers in Apostolic truth scattered through almost every country of Europe prior to the age of Luther (Mosheim 685).

Long before the dawn of the Reformation proper, many of these different independent movements and religious societies asserted themselves more strongly with the decline of papal influence and power. Some of these undoubtedly contained remnants of believers in Apostolic truth, now long languishing in an obscurity forced upon them by periodic persecutions and ravishments.

Among these, the Albigenses or Cathari, "puritans," grew to prominence in southern France around the year 1170. The Cathari made great use of Scripture, although they are reputed to have rejected parts of the Old Testament (Walker 250).

They translated and circulated copies of the New Testament, repudiated the authority of tradition, and attacked the Roman Catholic doctrines of purgatory, image worship, and various priestly claims. Their doctrine seems to have been a mixture of truth and error, but their rejection of papal authority brought forth a "crusade" against them at the behest of Pope Innocent III, in 1208. As a result, the sect was almost eradicated by the wanton slaughter of most of the inhabitants of the area, including many Catholics (Hurlbut 141).

The Waldenses

Another scattered group of believers in Apostolic teachings and practices were called Waldenses. Mosheim tells us how the Waldenses "multiplied and spread with amazing rapidity through all the countries of Europe, nor could they be exterminated entirely by any punishments, whether by death or any other forms of persecution" (Mosheim 429).

Unquestionably, there were different elements among those denominated as Waldenses. Some held to more Apostolic truth than others. Some, we are informed, "looked upon the Romish church as a real church of Christ, though greatly corrupted." But others "maintained that the church of Rome had apostatized from Christ, was destitute of the Holy Spirit, and was that Babylonian harlot mentioned by St. John" (Mosheim 430). As we have already seen, the enemies of these scattered Christian groups have often charged them falsely as to doctrines, and much of the scriptural truth they may have held has probably been lost with the destruction of their original writings. Yet even their enemies sometimes bear eloquent testimony as to the morals and doctrine of the Waldenses. As quoted in an appendix of Wharey's *Church History*, the following incident, taken from an early and reputed source, is indicative of the faith and practice of the early Waldenses:

> King Louis XII having received information from the enemies of the Waldenses, dwelling in Provence, of several heinous crimes which they fathered upon them, sent to the place Monsieur Adam Fumee, Master of Requests, and a certain Sorbonnist Doctor, called Parui, who was his confessor, to inquire into the matter. They visited all their parishes and temples, and neither found there any images, or sign of the ornaments belonging to the mass, or ceremonies of the Romish Church. Much less could they discover any of those crimes with which they were charged. But rather, that they kept the Sabbath duly; caused their children to be baptized according to the primitive Church; taught them the articles of the Christian faith, and the commandments of God. The king, having heard the report of the said commissioners, said, with an oath, that they were better men than himself or his people (Perrin 36).

Thus, it is evident that *much* knowledge of the "faith once for all delivered" existed in the minds of many faithful men and women throughout the Middle Ages. They were often gathered together in religious bodies for purposes of worship. Though sometimes scattered and persecuted, they were, in actual fact a *Church,* which carried on in the spirit, faith, and practice of Christ and His Apostles.

We need to consider the fact that the knowledge of Apostolic truth and practice, which they held, was available to Luther and the other reformers if they had desired it.

Besides these scattered groups of believers that had existed—*independent of Rome*—for hundreds of years, there were many individual leaders *within* the Roman Church who became alarmed at the spiritual decay and called for reform before the Reformation proper.

The Work of John Wycliffe

One of the most notable reformers before the Reformation was John Wycliffe, born about 1324 in Yorkshire, England. He is commonly called "the morning star of the Reformation."

At Oxford, he rose to scholarly distinction and eventually became a doctor of theology, holding several honorable positions at the university. He soon became a leader among those attempting to combat a number of glaring abuses of the clergy.

Wycliffe attacked the mendicant friars, the system of monasticism, and eventually opposed the authority of the pope in England. He also wrote against the doctrine of transubstantiation and advocated a simpler church service, according to the New Testament pattern.

He taught that the Scriptures are the only law of the Church. Yet he did not utterly reject the papacy, but only what he regarded as its abuse (Walker 299).

The incompetence of the clergy led him to send forth preachers, his "poor priests," wandering two by two throughout the country—to labor wherever there was need. Their success was great because there was already a strong resentment of foreign papal taxation and a longing to return to a more biblical faith.

Wycliffe Taught Obedience to the Ten Commandments

Although he never fully developed his doctrine and was very much enmeshed from birth with the Roman Catholic concepts of his time, Wycliffe clearly perceived the need to restore obedience to the Ten Commandments. He never employed the characteristic devices of the later reformers in evading this Apostolic doctrine. The learned historian, Augustus Neander, describes this frank approach. He states that one of Wycliffe's first works as a reformer...

>...was a detailed exposition of the Ten Commandments, in which he contrasted the immoral life prevalent among all ranks, in his time, with what these commandments require. We should undoubtedly keep in mind what he tells himself, that he was led to do this by the ignorance which most people betrayed of the decalogue; and that it was his design to counteract a tendency, which showed greater concern for the opinions of men than the law of God. But at the same time we cannot fail to perceive an inclination to adopt in whole the Old Testament form of the law, which shows itself in his applying the law of the Sabbath to the Christian observance of Sunday (Neander 9: 200–201).

It was perhaps unfortunate that Wycliffe left no follower of conspicuous ability to carry on his work in England. But his translation of the Bible into the English language, completed between 1382 and 1384, rendered a great and lasting benefit to his contemporaries. "The greatest service which he did the English people was his translation of the Bible, and his open defence of their right to read the Scriptures in their own tongue" (Fisher, *The History of the Christian Church* 274).

Although his opinions were condemned by the Roman hierarchy, attempts to imprison him proved ineffectual because of his friends and followers, and he was allowed to retire to his parish at Lutterworth, where he died a natural death. With his death, the political significance of the Lollard movement, as it was popularly called, came to an end. Mainly in secret, some of his followers remained active until the Reformation.

But his writings and teachings had gone abroad, and, as a historian states, "Wyclif's chief influence was to be in Bohemia rather than in the land of his birth" (Walker, Williston 301).

The Hussite Revival

That Wycliffe's views found a readier acceptance in Bohemia than they had in England was almost altogether due to the efforts of John Huss.

Huss was born in Bohemia in 1369, and was an ardent student of Wycliffe's writings, and preached most of his doctrines, especially those directed against papal encroachments. As rector of the University of Prague, Huss early held a commanding influence in Bohemia.

At first, he apparently hoped to reform the church from within, and had the confidence of his ecclesiastical superiors. But as a preacher, he denounced the prevailing sins of the clergy with great zeal, and began to arouse suspicion. When he was appointed to investigate some of the alleged miracles of the church, he ended up pronouncing them spurious and told his followers to quit looking for signs and wonders and to search the Scriptures instead.

At last, "his impassioned condemnation of the iniquitous sale of indulgences called down upon him the papal excommunication" (Fisher, *The History of the Church* 275). He was then persuaded by the sympathetic king to go into exile. But, unfortunately, he later agreed to appear before the Council of Constance after having received a pledge of safe conduct from the emperor. He defended his teachings as in accord with Scripture, but he was condemned by the council and delivered over to the civil power for execution. This method was always used so as to preserve the "innocence" of the Roman church in such matters.

The emperor's "safe conduct" pledge was broken upon the Catholic principle that "faith was not to be kept with heretics" (Hurlbut 143). The cruel sentence passed upon Huss was that he was to be burned at the stake. His courageous death, and that a year later of Jerome of Prague, who shared his reforming spirit and ideals, aroused the reforming element in Bohemia and influenced his countrymen for many years to come (Fisher, *The History of the Church* 276).

Jerome Savonarola

About 1452 was born at Florence, Italy, a man who was to challenge the papal corruptions in its own territory.

This man was Jerome Savonarola, who had become so disgusted with the wickedness and debauchery about him that he became a monk of the Dominican order partly in an effort to escape the evils all around him.

He preached violently against the ecclesiastical, social, and political evils of his day—sparing no age, sex, or condition of men. At first the city would not listen, but later filled the cathedral to overflowing. He no longer used reasonings in his sermons, but preached in the name of the Most High (Fisher, *The History of the Church* 276).

For a time, he effected a seeming reformation of the city, and became for a short time the virtual political and religious ruler of the city of Florence. But his political policy made him bitter enemies, among them the pope, Alexander VI. Refusing to keep his silence, Savonarola was soon excommunicated, seized, and imprisoned. After a prejudicial trial, he was hanged, then burned, and his ashes were thrown into the Arno River.

Historians agree that Savonarola's interests lay much less in doctrinal reforms than in the purification of morals. This was to be accomplished *within* the pale of the Roman Church. And we may note that, to a great extent, this was the case also with Wycliffe and Huss. All three had been reared Catholics in faith, practice, and outlook. With the possible exception of Wycliffe, all died as Catholics in actual fact—even though they sought a reformation *within* that body.

Thus, it is evident that no ordinary man, be he ever so able and zealous, would have been able to bring about a purification of the spiritual depravity of the Roman Catholic Church as a whole. As a result of the progress of papal power, the pope and his immediate court were the only ones who could do this.

Obstacles to a True Reformation

But the involvements of the iniquitous system were so great, the selling of ecclesiastical posts so rampant, the temptations to capitalize on the sale of indulgences and other church revenue so abundant, that even a sincere reformer within the papal court would have found his lot a hopeless one.

When men had sunk their whole fortune in buying a lucrative post, which had been put up for auction, would it not be monstrous to abolish all such posts? And there was no money with which to make compensation. When Leo X died, the papacy was not only in debt, but bankrupt. A reforming Pope had no chance of success. Every door was barred, and every wheel was jammed (Plummer 15).

Yet throughout the nations of Europe, there were many political, social, and economic abuses that cried out for reform—not to speak of the overwhelming religious abuses. One way or another, as we shall soon see, some sort of universal upheaval was inescapably destined to rock the outward complacency of that time.

But, as we have seen, the very men who tried to reform this corrupt system were so thoroughly indoctrinated with the teachings of Rome that it was most difficult to break completely away. We need to bear in mind that these men—and Luther, Zwingli, Calvin, and their associates—had *all* been reared from childhood in Roman Catholic doctrine and practice. They had been taught nothing else, and since there were practically no religious books or Bibles available in the common tongues, they knew of little else than the Roman Catholic faith, ceremonies, rituals, and traditions.

Therefore, it was virtually *impossible* for them to objectively look at the religious system in which they had been reared and compare it to the beliefs and practices of Jesus Christ and the inspired New Testament Church.

However, from a spiritual point of view, the real question of the hour was not whether there would be *some kind* of reformation, but whether there would be a return to the "faith once for all delivered." A return to the genuine *Christianity of the Apostles* was sorely needed. A return to the *true Gospel* and to the *faith* and *practice* of Christ and the Church as He founded it would have ushered in a new era of righteousness and worship, of peace and of joy.

Was such a *true* reformation forthcoming? This is the question that should burn itself into the minds and hearts of all thinking men and women, because the final answer to this question will determine—to a great extent—the real meaning of the religious division and confusion of our time.

The *answers* to these vital questions, the *unraveling* of this fascinating mystery, will appear in the next chapter.

Chapter 2

Setting the Stage for Revolution

W e have seen the startling fact that a *radical change* came over nominal "Christianity" soon after the days of the original Apostles. *Pagan* ceremonies, customs and traditions were quickly accepted into the professing Christian Church. And we have learned of the *corruption* and *debauchery* of the Catholic Church during the Middle or "Dark" Ages. We learned how men like Wycliffe, Huss and Savonarola were *unable* to purge this wickedness from *within* the organized church of their day. Many *paid with their lives!*

Now let us consider the real factors that caused men to *revolt* against the authority of the Roman Catholic Church. Again, let us ask ourselves these questions: Was this a sincere, Spirit-motivated return to the "faith once for all delivered to the saints"?

Immediate Causes of the Reformation

Many modern Protestants have assumed that the Reformation was purely a *religious* movement. They see visions of multitudes of sincere men throughout Germany and Europe wholeheartedly seeking a return to Apostolic faith and practice.

But this is not an accurate picture.

It is an historical fact that there were many selfish and materialistic reasons why the Reformation took place when and how it did. Many of them were entirely divorced from a purely religious motive.

There is no doubt that political, intellectual and financial considerations played a prominent part in bringing about the Reformation of the sixteenth century. A rising sense of nationalism caused men to feel that, as Germans, Frenchmen or Englishmen, they had common interests against all foreigners, even the pope himself.

As the cities of Europe grew in size and influence, the increased education, wealth and political influence of the middle class prepared them to play a decisive role in the coming upheaval. They began to grow restive under the constant ecclesiastical interference in temporal affairs (Walker, Reginald 289).

Coupled with this national feeling, the growth of absolutism had made the various rulers feel more independent of the See of Rome, and they often attempted to secure unfettered control of ecclesiastical appointments within their realms. This was the beginning of a tendency that later culminated in state-controlled churches in many lands. The marked friendship between the popes and the kings of France during the Avignon period gave rise to a general suspicion of papal motives in other nations. This scandal was heightened by the increase in papal taxation during this period, when "the removal of the papacy to Avignon largely cut off the revenues from the papal estates in Italy without diminishing the luxury or expensiveness of the papal court" (Walker, Reginald 292, 296).

Many complaints were voiced, not only by individuals, but by the most powerful kings and by whole nations, against the imperious domination of the popes, the frauds, violence, avarice and injustice of Rome. The insolence and tyranny of papal legates, along with the crimes, ignorance and moral depravity of priests and monks, made men everywhere wish for a reformation of the church "in its head and members" (Mosheim 24).

Acting in concert with all these forces was that remarkable movement known as the Renaissance, or the awakening of Europe to a new interest in science, literature and art. It was a movement that brought the change from medieval to modern ideals, culture and methods of thought.

If we are to understand the reformation that followed, we must first examine the interplay and action of each of these factors that played such an important part in its direction and final outcome.

Political and Financial Causes for Reform

As we have seen, papal power reached its height under Hildebrand (1073–1085), who, even more than his predecessors, aimed at the complete subordination of the "Holy Roman Empire" to the Roman church. The prosecution of this enterprise caused a protracted struggle for power between the papacy and the empire. In this struggle, the popes had great advantages over the emperors—whose actual dominions were far from equivalent to the area dominated by the church. One very effective support was found in the disposition of the German princes themselves to put checks upon the power of the emperors. And in the crusades the popes had the opportunity to direct the religious enthusiasm of the common people in all nations (Fisher, *The Reformation* 26–28).

Eventually, the papacy was triumphant in this struggle and the penitent Emperor, Henry IV, was forced to humble himself before Pope Hildebrand in order to retain the allegiance of his subjects. Thus, we behold the spectacle of the *church ruling over the state* and dictating its will to kings and emperors.

Indeed, the church had long dominated the empire to some extent, but never so completely.

In the eighteen years (1198–1216) in which Innocent III reigned, the papal institution shone forth in full splendor. The enforcement of celibacy had placed the entire body of the clergy in a closer relation to the sovereign pontiff. The Vicar of Peter had become the Vicar of God and of Christ... The king was to the Pope as the moon to the sun—a lower luminary shining with borrowed light (Fisher, *The Reformation* 29–30).

Thus, we see that the popes were making themselves out to be *God on earth*. They taught that Jesus Christ was setting up His millennial reign on earth *through them*.

However, before this papal power could long be exercised, it became evident that there were **new forces** rising in Europe to challenge its supremacy. In many lands, the patriotism of the people was resulting in an unwillingness to submit to foreign domination over their own national churches and a reluctance to pay "Peter's pence" for the construction of magnificent cathedrals in Rome (Hurlbut 118).

Abuse of Religious Office

In the exercise of its political and financial power, the Catholic church was riding for a fall. The popes seemed to have an insatiable craving for money. This wealth was not only used to further their quest of voluptuous and easy living, but to purchase *friends* and *power*. The Roman pontiffs were able to extract this money from their unwary subjects by various means concealed under the appearance of religion. Mosheim describes this abuse of power:

> Among these artifices, what were called indulgences—that is, liberty to buy off the punishments of their sins by contributing money to pious uses—held a distinguished place. And to these, recourse was had as often as the papal treasury became exhausted, to the immense injury of the public interests. Under some plausible, but for the most part false pretext, the ignorant and timorous people were beguiled with the prospect of great advantage by the hawkers of indulgences, who were in general base and profligate characters (Mosheim 88).

These scandals provided a very adequate reason in the eyes of many German princes, for instance, to throw off the papal yoke—whether by "reform" or revolt—in order to free themselves from papal taxation and interference, and to seize the wealth of the churches and monasteries. Luther's later attack on the papal financial policy and taxation instantly made him a champion of the German middle class and, indirectly, of all his countrymen, who had long harbored feelings of resentment toward the crafty and easy-living Italians.

In England, relatively the same situation prevailed. King Henry VIII had squandered most of the royal treasury inherited from his more astute father. At the same time, there was growing discontent among the nobles in particular with regard to excessive papal taxation, and the abundant wealth of the monastic orders would be prize pickings if the papal authority were cast off. It is significant that one of Henry's first actions after having himself recognized as the "supreme head of the Church and clergy of England" was to order the *confiscation* of the wealth of the church, particularly that of the monastic orders.

Through royal negligence and extravagance, there arose a class of sharers in the monastic loot whose vested interests lay in continued separation from the Church of Rome. This faction was a powerful guarantee against any later movements for reconciliation with the papacy (Walker, Reginald 56).

In view of these many temptations, and the nationalistic tendency already underway, it should have been the primary interest of the popes to reconcile the political and financial objections of the various nations. But such was *not* the case.

While the papacy should have been doing everything possible to avoid aggravating the peoples of Europe with its ruthless financial policy, it did just the opposite. Popes often used the wealth they received from indulgences and the sale of church offices to enrich their own relatives or to strengthen the states of the Roman church.

Fisher describes the wretched character of some of these popes:

> Innocent VIII, besides advancing the fortunes of seven illegitimate children, and waging two wars with Naples, received an annual tribute from the Sultan for detaining his brother and rival in prison, instead of sending him to lead a force against the Turks, the enemies of Christendom. Alexander VI, whose wickedness brings to mind the dark days of the Papacy in the tenth century, occupied himself in building up a principality for his favorite son, that monster of depravity, Caesar Borgia, and in amassing treasures, by base and cruel means, for the support of the licentious Roman Court. He is said to have died of the poison which he caused to be prepared for a rich cardinal, who bribed the head cook to set it before the Pope himself (Fisher, *The Reformation* 44–45).

Thus, it is evident that when the reformers began their pleas for a break with the papal authority, the wide response was often not so much from sincere religious motives as from the practical and natural desire of many to appropriate to themselves the political and financial rewards hitherto withheld or controlled by the Roman church.

The Renaissance

Another important factor in preparing the way for the Reformation was the revival of learning, literature and art called the Renaissance. The leaders of this movement were not usually priests or monks, but laymen. It opened as a literary movement and was not yet openly anti-religious, but only skeptical and inquiring. It was greatly aided by the invention of printing in 1455, by Gutenberg. For the first time, books could now be disseminated by the thousands, and it is significant that the first book printed was the Bible.

The Renaissance stimulated patriotism and served to inspire the production of a national literature. It encouraged independence in thought and national policies, and led to the development of the modern European nationalistic concepts as we know them. As strong national governments arose, this naturally tended to curb the authority of what had been regarded as the universal church. The influence of the pope and clergy became more and more limited to the religious sphere, and the diplomatic policy of each nation pursued a more independent course.

Increased interest in the pagan classics exerted a marked influence upon the educated classes, and caused them to break with medieval scholasticism, and, in many cases, with all serious concern with religion as such.

The medieval ideals had been otherworldly and encouraged self-abnegation. The Renaissance introduced humanism and the expression of the inherent tendencies in man. The attitude of ascetic seclusion gave way to the search for full enjoyment of all the world can offer.

A rational search into the history and literature of the past subjected many documents of the church to critical examination. A school of historical criticism was started by Lorenzo Valla (1405–1457), who exposed the falsity of the Donation of Constantine and denied the Apostolic origin of the Apostle's Creed. All this inquiry and revival of human interests served to undermine the authority and influence of the Catholic church.

For about two generations before the Protestant Reformation, the popes themselves tried to enter into the spirit of the Renaissance, and the popes of that time were marked by culture rather than religious faith. This naturally resulted in the papal court becoming even more worldly, and brought about an increased demand for a reformation of the church.

"One very beneficial result of the Renaissance was the revived interest in the study of Hebrew and Greek. This promoted a better understanding of the Bible on which the great reformatory work of Luther, Zwingli, and Calvin was based. Without this preparation their work would not have been possible" (Qualben 199).

Perhaps the most outstanding Renaissance scholar was Desiderius Erasmus, who had been accused of "laying the egg that Luther hatched." He studied in several different European nations. Although he was primarily a Roman Catholic, his provocative satires of the clerical abuses of his time and his appeal to return to the simplicity of original Christianity had a profound effect on the educated classes of his time, and, through them, reached the masses of Europe's people.

Erasmus was convinced that the Roman system was filled with superstition and corruption. Yet he had no wish to break with Catholicism. He looked upon it, sentimentally, as the "mother" of society and the arts. And he was too intellectual to sympathize with the Lutheran revolt, the brutal excesses of which repelled him.

> Hence neither side in the struggle that opened in the latter part of his life understood him, and his memory has been condemned by polemic writers, Protestant and Catholic. His own thought was that education, return to the sources of Christian truth, and flagellation of ignorance and immorality by merciless satire would bring the church to purity. To this end he labored (Walker, Reginald 329).

Thus, we find that the humanists helped prepare the way for the Reformation. They discredited much of the Catholic theology. They encouraged men to study the Bible and early church writers from a new point of view. They helped release the minds of men from medieval traditionalism, and began an era of independent scholarship and thinking centered around the desires and needs of man.

With the rise of nationalism, the invention of printing and increased distribution of knowledge, this intellectual movement would have eventually brought about tremendous changes in medieval Catholicism and in the freedom of the individual, even had there been no Luther, Zwingli or Calvin. So, when the Reformation did begin, it was helped to success by forces that were purely intellectual and often irreligious in nature.

Religious Abuses Calling for Reform

The details of the degenerate morals and ecclesiastical corruption in the period immediately preceding the Reformation are so well-known that they need only brief summarization and analysis here. However, a vitally important question arises—one that is usually overlooked or pushed aside. That is the fundamental question of *whether* the paganized, radically changed and corrupted religio-political machine dominating the nations of Europe, called the Roman Catholic Church, was in actual fact the rightful and legitimate successor of the original Apostolic Church—the *one true Church* Jesus Christ said He would build.

For, as we shall later see, the Protestant churches, as a whole, base their claim of historic unity with the Apostolic Church upon their direct descendance from the Roman Catholic Church, their "mother" church.

Was this church the Church Jesus built? Were its leaders and its members filled with, and led by the *Spirit of God*? This is a vital point, for as the Apostle Paul states: "Now if anyone does not have the Spirit of Christ, *he is not His*" (Romans 8:9).

We can do no better than draw our conclusions from the statements of recognized historians in this field. A direct comparison is made by Plummer:

> And as soon as the revival of letters caused the contents of the New Testament and the teaching of the Fathers to be known, it was seen that what passed for Christianity at the close of the fifteenth century was scarcely recognizable as such, when placed side by side with what we know of Christianity at the close of the Apostolic Age (Plummer 11).

A picturesque and comprehensive description of this state of things as it affected the daily lives of the people is given by the noted historian D'Aubigne:

> Let us now see what was the state of the Church previous to the Reformation. The nations of Christendom no longer looked to a holy and living God for the free gift of eternal life. To obtain it, they were obligated to have recourse to all the means that a superstitious, fearful, and alarmed imagination could devise. Heaven was filled with saints and mediators, whose duty it was to solicit this mercy. Earth was filled with pious works, sacrifices, observances, and ceremonies, by which it was to be obtained (D'Aubigne 17).

Christ was depicted as a *stern judge*, prepared to condemn anyone who did not invoke the intercession of the saints or resort to the papal indulgences.

Many intercessors appeared in Christ's place. First was the Virgin Mary, like the Diana of paganism, and then the saints—whose numbers were continually augmented by the popes.

Religious pilgrimages were prescribed as a penance for sin. There were almost as many religious resorts for pilgrims as there were mountains, forests and valleys. On these pilgrimages, the people brought to the priests money and anything that had any value—fowls, ducks, geese, wax, straw, butter and cheese.

D'Aubigne continues:

> The bishops no longer preached, but they consecrated priests, bells, monks, churches, chapels, images, books, and cemeteries; and all this brought in a large revenue. Bones, arms, and feet were preserved in gold and silver boxes; they were given out during mass for the faithful to kiss, and this too was a source of great profit. All these people maintained that the pope, "sitting as God in the temple of God," could not err, and they would not suffer any contradiction (D'Aubigne 17).

It is related that in the very church where Luther preached at Wittenberg, was shown a supposed fragment of Noah's ark, a piece of wood from the cradle of Jesus, some hair from the beard of St. Christopher, and nineteen thousand other relics.

These religious relics were hawked about the countryside and sold to the faithful for the spiritual merits they were supposed to bestow. The wandering salesmen paid a percentage of their profits to the original owners of the relics. "The kingdom of heaven had disappeared, and in its place a market of abominations had been opened upon earth" (D'Aubigne 17).

The Debauched Clergy

If the members of this professing Christendom may be partially excused due to prevailing ignorance and lack of right spiritual guidance, such excuses carry no weight when applied to the higher clergy and to the popes themselves. For these men had every advantage of education and knowledge, *if* they had rightly desired to apply such advantages.

The deplorable corruption of the Roman church during the century just before the Reformation is appalling. Many of the popes were no more than "respectable" gangsters.

No *trace* of the Holy Spirit of God is to be found in their words or actions. Yet they *headed* and *represented* what was supposed to be the only Church of God on earth!

Regarding two of these popes, Wharey states:

> Sixtus IV had sixteen illegitimate children, whom he took special care to provide for, and enrich. But of all the popes of this age, perhaps Roderic Borgia, who assumed the name of Alexander VI, excelled in wickedness. He has been called the Catiline of the popes; and the villainies, crimes, and enormities recorded of him, are so many and so great, that it must be certain that he was destitute, not only of all religion, but also of decency and shame (Wharey 211–12).

It was a common practice in those times for the priests to pay the price of blackmail to their bishops for the illegal concubines with whom they shared their beds, and for each illegitimate child thus produced (D'Aubigne 18). The Roman religion no longer contained anything that would cause it to be esteemed by those who were truly pious, and nearly the whole worship of God consisted in outward paganized ceremonies. Such sermons as were occasionally addressed to the people were not only destitute of all taste and good sense, but were stuffed with fables and nauseous fictions (Mosheim 547).

Had God's True Church Become Corrupted?

And yet, after themselves relating these accounts of the spiritual stench, utter depravity of morals, and total ignorance or disregard for all Christian truth and virtue that characterized the Roman church for many generations, these very Protestant writers attempt in the next breath to label this reprobate system the "Church of Christ"—the Church Jesus said He would build, the Spirit-filled body of which He is the *living* Head! (Ephesians 1:22).

Notice D'Aubigne's pitiful lament: "The evil had spread through all ranks: 'a strong delusion' had been sent among men; the corruption of manners corresponded with the corruption of faith. A mystery of iniquity oppressed *the enslaved Church of Christ*" (D'Aubigne 20).

Of the fact that a purifying and cleaning up of this society was needed, there is no doubt, but of the supposed fact that this *totally paganized* system was the Church of God on earth, there is *great doubt.*

In fact, the description of the true Church as given in the New Testament is in *total contradiction* to the faith, practice, and life of Roman Catholicism as it has existed for hundreds of years!

The inspired command of Peter to *repent* and be *baptized* (Acts 2:38) was replaced by the Roman injunction to "do penance"—confess to and pay money to the priest. The Apostolic way of life of *love* and *obedience* to God's spiritual laws was replaced by a pattern of *fear* and a superstitious observance of special fasts, feasts and church festivals utterly foreign to Christ and the early true Church.

In place of the inspired form of Church government instituted by Christ and carried on by the Apostles, we find a corrupt hierarchy of priestly offices, which are not so much as mentioned in the Bible. And over the whole corrupted system we find the Roman pope, who would sit "as God in the temple of God" (2 Thessalonians 2:4), often disobedient himself to all the laws of God and man, yet holding forth with authority as the "Vicar of Christ," and permitting and encouraging men to prostrate themselves before him in a kind of worship that Peter and the other Apostles would have feared to allow (Acts 10:25–26).

Was this utterly debased religio-political system the legitimate descendant of the Church Jesus and the Apostles founded? Would a "reformation" of *this* foul system constitute a continuation of the true Church?

These are the really *basic* questions that we need to consider. And let us not hide our eyes from the inescapable fact that it was *directly* from the Roman Catholic system that the Protestant churches have sprung.

As we have now seen, political, economic, social, intellectual and religious factors throughout the nations of Europe presaged a universal upheaval. And *political* and *financial* considerations played a very important part in the coming reformation.

When it came, what was its true significance in the overall *plan* and *purpose* of the eternal God? Was it a recapturing of the "faith once for all delivered" to the saints? We need to face these questions squarely.

In the next chapter, we will deal directly with the beginning of the Protestant Reformation under Martin Luther. Many of the *hidden facts* about *what* actually took place and *why* are truly eye-opening!

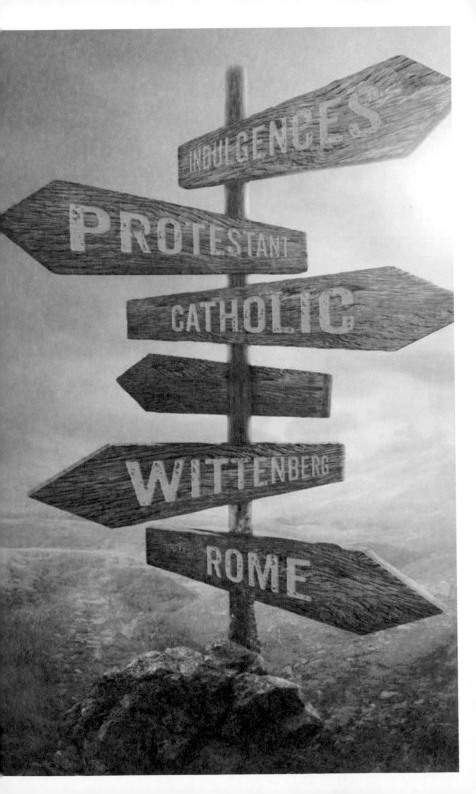

Chapter 3

The Break with Rome

Millions of Protestant books, pamphlets and tracts boldly proclaim as the Protestant foundation, "The Bible, the whole Bible, and nothing but the Bible, is the religion of Protestants."

In the first two chapters, we learned from the Bible and the record of history that a remarkable *change* took place in nominal Christianity soon after the death of the original Apostles. *Pagan* ceremonies, traditions, and ideas were introduced into the professing Christian church. Later, we found that during the "Dark" ages that followed, the corruption and worldliness of the ruling Catholic church led professing Christians of that era to superstitious beliefs and observances that would have shocked Peter or Paul!

We have asked: Was the Protestant movement a reformation of God's true Church gone wrong? *Did* the Protestant reformers restore "the faith which was once for all delivered to the saints"? Was this movement inspired and guided by God's Holy Spirit? Do the "fruits" prove this?

Now we will come directly to the beginning of the actual Reformation under Martin Luther.

Luther's Revolt Against Rome

As we have seen, on the eve of the Reformation there were many complaints and abuses that called for reform. Those who were responsible for the spiritual and material welfare of the people were content to preserve the status quo, because it served their own enrichment and religious or political advantage.

Yet the people cried out for *financial relief*—for at least some measure of *political freedom*—and the yoke of *religious oppression* lay heavily on the populace of Europe.

Some *outstanding personality* was needed to sound the cry of alarm, which would inevitably set off a universal explosion that had long been smoldering. Yet no ordinary leader, no matter what his ideals or personal brilliance, could fulfill this role. It would take someone who could identify himself with the unspoken cravings of the local princes, the middle classes, the peasants—someone who could uniquely identify himself with their long-suffered grievances, and so become a symbol of the universal urge for a complete revolution in the religious, social, and political life of that day.

Such a man was Martin Luther.

The complete identification of Luther with the Protestant Reformation, the uniqueness of his personality as its center and rallying point, is attested to by all historians. Historian George Fisher describes this circumstance: "Unquestionably the hero of the Reformation was Luther. Without him and his powerful influence, other reformatory movements, even such as had an independent beginning, like that of Zwingli, might have failed of success... Luther apart from the Reformation would cease to be Luther" (Fisher, *The Reformation* 87).

An understanding of the basic facts concerning Luther's childhood and youthful life is important as a background to an adequate comprehension of his later beliefs and doctrines.

Luther's Early Life

Martin Luther was born at Eisleben, Germany, in 1483, the son of a peasant. The family moved to Mansfield six months after Luther's birth and he was brought up there in an atmosphere of austerity and disciplined virtue.

An intimate glimpse is given into Luther's early home and school life in Roland Bainton's definitive biography:

> Luther is reported to have said, "My mother caned me for
> stealing a nut, until the blood came. Such strict discipline

drove me to the monastery, although she meant it well." This
saying is reinforced by two others: "My father once whipped
me so that I ran away and felt ugly toward him until he was
at pains to win me back." "[At school] I was caned in a single
morning fifteen times for nothing at all. I was required
to decline and conjugate and hadn't learned my lesson"
(Bainton 7–8.).

Even in these early glimpses, we can see a pattern of incidents
that eventually led Luther to want to *escape* authority and any need
for *obedience*. We need to understand his background of medieval *superstition* and *fear* in order to fully understand his emphasis on faith
alone in later years.

The atmosphere of Luther's family was decidedly that of rugged
peasantry. But there was a strong religious feeling in the family, and
his father, Hans, prayed at the bedside of his son, and his mother was
known in the community as a very devout person.

Yet many elements of old German paganism were blended with
"Christian" mythology in the beliefs of the peasants. The woods,
they thought, were peopled by elves, gnomes, fairies, witches, and
other spirits. Luther's own mother believed them capable of stealing
eggs, milk, and butter. Luther himself retained many of these beliefs
until his death. He once said: "In my native country on the top of a
high mountain called the Pubelsberg is a lake into which if a stone be
thrown a tempest will arise over the whole region because the waters
are the abode of captive demons" (Bainton 19). His early Catholic religious life was filled with scenes of steeples, spires, cloisters, priests,
monks of various orders, collections of relics, ringing of bells, pro-
claiming of indulgences, religious processions, and supposed cures at
shrines. In all these things, he had a normal religious upbringing for
those days.

At fifteen, Luther was sent to school at Eisenach, where his
mother had relatives. As did many of the other poor students there,
he was obliged to sing in the streets, begging for bread. In 1501,
Luther went to the University of Erfurt, having agreed with his father to study for a legal career. While still a student there, a number
of spiritual crises upset Luther's course, and eventually redirected
his entire life.

Luther's Own Spiritual Upheaval

Before relating the specific events that led Luther to depart from the ordinary life that his father had planned for him, it will be helpful to notice the effect that the normal religious training of that age had on youths in general, and on Luther in particular.

> There is just one respect in which Luther appears to have been different from other youths of his time, namely, in that he was extraordinarily sensitive and subject to recurrent periods of exaltation and depression of spirit. This oscillation of mood plagued him throughout his life. He testified that it began in his youth and that the depressions had been acute in the six months prior to his entry into the monastery (Bainton 20).

We can see that Luther had a very troubled mind indeed. This problem of moodiness—aggravated by a feeling of perpetual *guilt*, which the Catholic doctrines engendered—made Luther seek a type of emotional release from these inner conflicts.

Bainton states:

> The explanation lies rather in the tensions which medieval religion deliberately induced, playing alternately upon fear and hope. Hell was stoked, not because men lived in perpetual dread, but precisely because they did not, and in order to instill enough fear to drive them to the sacraments of the church. If they were petrified with terror, purgatory was introduced by way of mitigation as an intermediate place where those not bad enough for hell nor good enough for heaven might make further expiation. If this alleviation inspired complacency, the temperature was advanced on purgatory, and then the pressure was again relaxed through indulgences (Bainton 21).

Thus, we can see that Luther's sensitivity was easily played upon by religious fears that had been inculcated since childhood. These fears were an integral part of the system that Luther eventually came to abhor.

Perhaps the first in a series of events that led Luther gradually to his eventual role as a reformer was a discovery he made when he was twenty years old and had already taken his Bachelor's degree. It happened that, while he was looking one day at the books in the Erfurt library, he casually picked up a copy of the Latin Bible. This was the *first time* that he had ever held a copy of the Bible in his hands, and he was surprised at the richness of its contents and studied it eagerly (Fisher, *The Reformation* 88). Although he had been for some time now engrossed in humanistic studies, on reading the Scriptures for the first time on this and subsequent occasions, the *deep religious anxieties* that had affected him from childhood returned and began to occupy his thoughts.

Thunder Strikes Luther

Later, returning to Erfurt from a visit with his parents, a storm arose and a thunderbolt struck down Luther and his companion. Luther quickly regained his feet, but was deeply moved when he discovered that his friend, Alexis, had been killed. Then and there, Luther determined to make his peace with God, and he soon entered the Augustinian monastery at Erfurt to become a priest.

In 1507, he was ordained to the priesthood, but his studies and spiritual exercises failed to bring him the inward peace he so desperately sought. He was encouraged to study passages from the Scriptures and the church fathers, by Staupitz, the vicar of the order. But this study, although helpful, did not quiet Luther's restlessness and inward torment.

During this time, many were struck by the *remarkable appearance* of Luther. In 1518, a contemporary said of him, "I could hardly look the man in the face, such a diabolical fire darted out of his eyes" (Hausser 8).

Luther Felt Unable to Obey God

Feeling a deep sense of personal *inadequacy* and *sin*, he set out to perform whatever good works were prescribed for the saving of his soul. And there were many such exercises recommended by the Catholicism of that day.

He fasted, sometimes three days on end without a crumb.
The seasons of fasting were more consoling to him than

those of feasting. Lent was more comforting than Easter. He laid upon himself vigils and prayers in excess of those stipulated by the rule. He cast off the blankets permitted him and well-nigh froze himself to death. At times he was proud of his sanctity and would say, "I have done nothing wrong today." Then misgivings would arise. "Have you fasted enough? Are you poor enough?" He would then strip himself of all, save that which decency required. He believed in later life that his austerities had done permanent damage to his digestion (Bainton 34).

All Luther knew of Christ at this time was that He was a "stern judge" from whom he would like to flee. Under a feeling of utter condemnation, Luther persisted in afflicting his body and mind with the various religious exercises practiced by the monks of his day. "If a monk ever won heaven by monkery, he has said, I would have found my way there also; all my convent comrades will bear witness to that" (Lindsay 427).

Notice that these things all indicate Luther's strong attachment to the Roman church. He was part and parcel with it, had been reared in it, steeped in its doctrines. And as is often the case in similar instances, when the break did come, it was to be a violent one.

The trouble was that he could not satisfy God at any point. Commenting in later life on the Sermon on the Mount, Luther gave searching expression to his disillusionment. Referring to the precepts of Jesus he said: "This word is too high and too hard that anyone should fulfill it. This is proved, not merely by our Lord's word, but by our own experience and feeling. Take any upright man or woman. He will get along very nicely with those who do not provoke him, but let someone proffer only the slightest irritation and he will flare up in anger... if not against friends, then against enemies. Flesh and blood cannot rise above it" (Bainton 34).

Determining in his own mind that it is *impossible* for man to perform what God requires, Luther continued his search for an answer to his *guilt complex*. Having been made a professor in the University of Wittenberg, which was operated in connection with the Augustinian monastery there, he began to lecture on the epistles of Paul.

He had hardly begun his exposition of the epistle to the Romans when his eyes fastened on the passage, *"The just shall live by faith"* (Romans 1:17). These words made a profound impression on Luther, and he pondered their meaning at great length.

His Disillusionment with the Papacy

When Luther visited Rome at some time during this period, he ran about the city full of devotional ardor, attempting to secure for himself the spiritual blessings that were offered by viewing various holy relics and doing penance at sacred shrines. While he did penance upon the stairs of the so-called judgment seat of Pilate, the haunting text of Scripture again entered his mind—"The just shall live by faith."

Throughout Luther's stay in Rome, disillusionment began to grow in his mind as to the character of the Roman church. He began to see what a *corrupt* and *abominable* system it had become. While officiating at several masses in Rome, he tried to maintain the dignity and reverence he felt this action required. But he was very disturbed at the frivolous and totally irreverent manner in which the Roman priests celebrated the sacrament of the altar. D'Aubigne relates:

> One day when he was officiating he found that the priests at an adjoining altar had already repeated seven masses before he had finished one. "Quick, quick!" cried one of them, "send our Lady back her Son;" making an impious allusion to the transubstantiation of the bread into the body and blood of Jesus Christ. At another time Luther had only just reached the Gospel, when the priest at his side had already terminated the mass. "Passa, passa!" cried the latter to him, "make haste! Have done with it at once" (D'Aubigne 193).

His astonishment was still greater, when he found in the *dignitaries of the papacy* what he had already observed in the inferior clergy. He had hoped better things of them" (D'Aubigne 68).

Returning home, he pondered over the scenes of the pious pilgrims in Rome seeking salvation through various endeavors. And he shuddered as he recalled the frivolity, the moral wretchedness, and the lack of real spiritual knowledge in that city—supposedly, "the capital of Christendom." The words of Paul returned to him again—"The just shall live by faith." At last he felt that he could understand them.

The Heart of Luther's Theology

Fisher notes of Luther:

> He saw that Christ is not come as a lawgiver, but as a Saviour; that love, not wrath or justice, is the motive in his mission and work; that the forgiveness of sins through Him is a free gift; that the relationship of the soul to Him, and through Him to the Father, which is expressed by the term *faith*, the responsive act of the soul to the divine mercy, *is all that is required*. This method of reconciliation is without the works of the law (Fisher, *The Reformation* 91).

Now we see the central point of all Luther's theology. This *doctrine of justification* became the *cornerstone* of all of Luther's subsequent religious efforts. *It alone had provided him with a sense of release from his haunting sense of guilt and fear of damnation*. And, we may truly add, it gave him a way *around* the requirements of *God's spiritual law*—which Luther felt he *could not keep*—and which he ultimately grew to *hate*.

It is evident that in all this thinking about law, Luther was substituting the Catholic idea of ritualistic "works" and *penances* for the Ten Commandments of God. *Obsessed* with the idea of getting around a need for any obedience, he began to feel that faith alone is sufficient for salvation.

The logical consequence of Luther's new position demanded a clash with Rome. It was on the question of the sale of *indulgences* that his direct opposition to orthodox Catholic doctrine was first made known.

The Doctrine of Indulgences

After his return from Rome, Luther had resumed his teaching career in the University of Wittenberg, and continued in his study of the

Scripture, and in the development of his theory of justification and salvation. Through the encouragement of his superior, Staupitz, he completed his work for his doctor's degree so that he might replace Staupitz by assuming the chair of Bible studies at the university. In 1512, he took the degree of Doctor of Divinity, and continued his teaching career.

All the while, his ideas on justification were growing and developing. He wrote:

> I greatly longed to understand Paul's Epistle to the Romans and nothing stood in the way but that one expression, "the justice of God," because I took it to mean that justice whereby God is just and deals justly in punishing the unjust. My situation was that, although an impeccable monk, I stood before God as a sinner troubled in conscience, and I had no confidence that my merit would assuage him. Therefore I did not love a just and angry God, but rather *hated* and *murmured against him*. Yet I clung to the dear Paul and had a great yearning to know what he meant (Bainton 49).

Notice that Luther confessed that he *hated* God in the role of Lawgiver and Judge. True enough, his false Catholic concept of obedience confused him as to the real spiritual issues at stake. He was like a man *spiritually drunk*—seeking his way out of an abyss. But in his mental torment from Catholic teaching, he was also desperately determined to find a *way around* obedience, law, and justice.

Luther wrote:

> Night and day I pondered until I saw the connection between the justice of God and the statement that "the just shall live by his faith." Then I grasped that the justice of God is that righteousness by which through grace and sheer mercy God justifies us through faith. Thereupon I felt myself to be reborn and to have gone through open doors into paradise. The whole of Scripture took on a new meaning, and whereas before the "justice of God" had filled me with hate, now it became to me inexpressibly sweet in greater love. This passage of Paul became to me a gate to heaven... (Bainton 49).

Thus, we can see that with the increasing stress Luther was putting on justification by faith *alone*, the Roman Catholic practice of selling *indulgences* for sin would be particularly distasteful to him—and an abuse he would naturally want to attack. Since the matter of *indulgences* was the immediate cause of Luther's break with Rome, it will be particularly helpful at this point to quote a scholarly description of this practice, and the exact wording of the indulgences.

Description of Indulgences

James Wharey documents the practice of indulgences in detail:

Indulgences, in the Romish church, are a remission of the punishment due to sin, granted by the church, and supposed to save the sinner from purgatory. According to the doctrine of the Romish church, all the good works of the saints, over and above those that were necessary for their own justification, are deposited, together with the infinite merits of Jesus Christ, in an inexhaustible treasury. The keys of this were committed to St. Peter, and to his successors, the popes, who may open it at pleasure; and, by transferring a portion of this superabundant merit to any particular person for a sum of money, may convey to him either the pardon of his own sins, or a release of any one for whom he is interested, from the pains of purgatory. Such indulgences were first invented in the eleventh century, by Urban II., as a recompense to those who went in person upon the glorious enterprise of conquering the Holy Land. They were afterwards granted to any one who hired a soldier for that purpose; and, in process of time, were bestowed on such as gave money for accomplishing any pious work enjoined by the pope. The power of granting indulgences has been greatly abused in the Church of Rome. Pope Leo X., in order to carry on the magnificent structure of St. Peter's at Rome, published indulgences, and a plenary permission to all such as should contribute money towards it. Finding the project take, he granted to Albert, elector of Mentz, and archbishop of Magdeburg, the benefit of the indulgences of Saxony, and the neighboring parts, and farmed out those of other countries to the highest bidders; who, to make the best of their bargain, procured the ablest preachers to cry up the value of the ware. The form of these indulgences was as follows:

"May our Lord Jesus Christ have mercy upon thee, and absolve thee by the merits of his most holy passion. And I, by his authority, that of his blessed apostles, Peter and Paul, and of the most holy pope, granted and committed to me in these parts, do absolve thee, first from all ecclesiastical censures, in whatever manner they have been incurred; then from all thy sins, transgressions, and excesses, how enormous soever they may be; even from such as are reserved for the cognizance of the holy see, and as far as the keys of the holy church extend. I remit to you all punishment which you deserve in purgatory on their account; and I restore you to the holy sacraments of the church, to the union of the faithful, and to the innocence and purity which you possessed at baptism; so that when you die, the gates of punishment shall be shut, and the gates of the paradise of delights shall be opened: and if you shall not die at present, this grace shall remain in full force when you are at the point of death. In the name of the Father, the Son, and the Holy Ghost" (Wharey 224–226).

Wharey notes that the glowing descriptions that the hawkers of indulgences gave of their benefits were sometimes almost incredible. If a man, they said, should purchase letters of indulgence, his soul may rest assured of its salvation. "Lo," they said, "the heavens are open; if you enter not now, when will you enter?"

It was the *great abuse* of this already abominable practice that led Martin Luther to take a definite stand against Rome. He was, of course, correct in opposing this practice. Taking the stand he took required courage. But the question we wish to consider is whether this led him to return to the "faith once for all delivered," or simply to reject that part of the Catholic teaching he could not agree with—and to set up in its place another purely *human*-inspired ecclesiastical system that suited *him*.

The Indulgence for St. Peter's in Rome

In Luther's vicinity, the proclamation of the indulgence to help rebuild St. Peter's in Rome was entrusted to a Dominican, Tetzel, an experienced vendor. The indulgence was not actually offered in

Luther's parish, because the church could not introduce an indulgence without the permission of the local authorities. In this case, the elector, Frederick the Wise, would not give his consent because he did not wish the indulgence of St. Peter's to encroach upon the indulgences of All Saints' Church at Wittenberg (Bainton 57).

But Tetzel came so close that Luther's parishioners could go over the border and return with some amazing concessions as a result of the high-pressure sales campaign Tetzel and his fellow hawkers were conducting.

Luther was righteously indignant at this shameless imposition of the pope, and his reformer's blood was roused. He drew up ninety-five theses for debate and nailed them to the door of the Castle Church at Wittenberg, as was the practice of the time for public posting. This was on October 31, 1517.

Many of Luther's theses appealed to the desperate financial straits of the German peasants, and indirectly appealed to the papacy to stop exacting more money from them. In his fiftieth proposition, Luther maintained: "Christians must be taught that if the pope knew the exactions of the preachers of indulgences, he would rather have St. Peter's basilica reduced to ashes, than built with the skin, flesh, and bones of his sheep" (Bettenson 267).

In the heated discussions that followed, Luther declared:

> The revenues of all Christendom are being sucked into
> this insatiable basilica. The Germans laugh at calling this
> the common treasure of *Christendom*. Before long all the
> churches, palaces, walls, and bridges of Rome will be built
> out of our money. First of all we should rear living temples,
> not local churches, and only last of all St. Peter's, which is
> not necessary for us. We Germans cannot attend St. Peter's.
> Better that it should never be built than that our parochial
> churches should be despoiled (Bainton 61).

Luther's *political appeal* to his fellow Germans is evident in all the early writings on this subject. He does not argue from the spiritual principle of what is right or wrong before God, but primarily from the *nationalistic* attitude that the money from indulgences should be spent on German religious causes.

Luther's attack on the papal financial policy brought a ready agreement among the Germans, who had long suffered from a sense of grievance against the *Italian* hierarchy—as they often regarded it. Luther's other point, that indulgences were spiritually harmful to the recipient, and that the pope has no absolute power over purgatory or the forgiveness of sins, also stirred up controversy.

Although the average German was likely to fully understand only the demand for financial relief, only Luther's connection of this popular grievance with the idea of blasphemy against the mercy of God would have the appeal to create a *popular revolution*.

Luther took no steps to spread his theses among the people. But others quietly translated them into German and had them printed. They soon became the talk of all Germany, and Luther's career as a reformer had been launched (Bainton 62–63).

Luther's Final Break with Rome

When Luther first posted his theses, he did not intend them for general dissemination. But now that they had been distributed, he stood by them in subsequent discussions and in tracts, which he wrote in their defense. Although news of these developments traveled slowly, it was not long before the authorities in Rome knew that the greater part of Germany was taking sides with Luther.

An accusation was brought against Luther at Rome, and the pope commissioned Cardinal Cajetan to represent him in talks with Luther. He was told to try to persuade Luther to give up any radical ideas—and to handle the affair with as little disturbance as possible (Hausser 19–20). But Cajetan's efforts changed nothing.

Thereupon, a second attempt was made to keep Luther within the Roman fold. Karl von Miltitz, a papal nuncio, was able to win Luther's confidence and make an agreement with him to maintain silence—provided his enemies would also—until papal representatives had been able to look into Luther's new doctrines. "And then," Luther said, "if I am convicted of error, I shall willingly retract it, and not weaken the power and glory of the holy Roman Church" (Hausser, 22).

We notice that Luther *still* regarded the Roman church as "holy"! It is important to realize how thoroughly *steeped* in her philosophies and doctrines Luther actually was. True, he eventually came to sharply disagree on several points. But to the very end, Martin Luther—born and reared a Roman Catholic, and a Catholic priest by profession—was literally *saturated* with the concepts, dogmas, and traditions that his church had accumulated through the Middle Ages.

As late as March 3, 1519, Luther wrote the pope:

> Now, Most Holy Father, I protest before God and his crea-tures that it has never been my purpose, nor is it now, to do ought that might weaken, or overthrow the authority of the Roman Church or that of your Holiness; nay, more, I confess that the power of this church is above all things; that nothing in heaven or on earth is to be set before it, Jesus alone, the Lord of all, excepted (Alzog 195).

Unless he were lying in this letter, Martin Luther—even at this late date—felt that the Roman Catholic religion was the true Church of God on earth!

Luther's Course of Action

But his truce with Rome not to speak out was to be short-lived. Dr. John Eck, a theologian from Leipzig, publicly challenged Luther to debate on his new doctrines (Hausser 22). So, the battle of words and pamphlets revived.

In the debates, Luther, as he always did, confused *justification* and *salvation*. He maintained that faith *alone*—without any works—suffices for salvation. When confronted with conflicting statements from the Epistle of James, *he called into question the authenticity of the epistle* (Alzog 302).

It is important to realize that not once, but *many times*, Luther would challenge the authority of any book in the Bible which seemed to disagree with *his ideas on justification*. We will discuss Luther's contradictory statements on the Holy Scripture later in this book.

After the Leipzig debates, Dr. Eck set out for Rome to warn Pope Leo X of the danger Luther was becoming to the Catholic Church in Germany. A papal bull was issued in 1520 condemning Luther and forty-one of his propositions. He himself was to be excommunicated if he did not retract within sixty days (Alzog 300).

Powerful Support Gathers

Because of Luther's popularity with both the common people and the nobility, the papal bull was received with open repugnance in Germany. Many declared that it was not necessary to obey it, and Luther's protector, Frederick the Wise, openly disclaimed obedience to the bull. Luther then took the unheard-of step of publicly burning the papal bull in the presence of his fellow monks, the students, and the citizens of Wittenberg (Hausser 27).

This bold step of making a complete break with Rome drew the attention of the entire German nation to Luther's cause. He quickly found *political support* in the friendly disposition of the elector and of the jurists who had a long-standing grievance over the interference of ecclesiastical courts in civil affairs. He also found ready allies in the humanist scholars who were filled with nationalistic fervor and were ready to avenge the indignities suffered by Germany under Italian and papal rule. They were ready to write with invective and satire—and also to use their swords (Fisher, *The Reformation* 102).

Soon after these events, Luther made a *political appeal* to the German nobility for their backing. His challenge to the "glorious Teutonic people" who were "born to be masters" had an electrifying effect on many of the German nobles and princes. But it was purely *political*, and this same type of appeal has been used with success by German generals and dictators of our more modern era, as well! Luther urged:

> Poor Germans that we are—we have been deceived! We were born to be masters, and we have been compelled to bow the head beneath the yoke of our tyrants, and to become slaves. Name, title, outward signs of royalty, we possess all these; force, power, right, liberty, all these have gone over to the popes, who have robbed us of them. They get the kernel, we get the husk... It is time the glorious Teutonic people should cease to be the puppet of the Roman pontiff" (Bettenson 278).

From here on, it remained for Luther and his adherents to attempt to found a *new religious system*, embracing the doctrines flowing from Luther's active pen. In future chapters, we will see if Luther's system constituted a return to the *faith, doctrine,* and *practice* of Christ and the Apostolic Church.

Chapter 4

The Reformation Grows

After his final break with Rome, Luther began to cultivate a number of the leading nobles and princes to support his cause. Without proper protection, he was a *dead man*—under the ban of the emperor and the pope.

During his disputes with John Eck, and in his preaching, writing, and other reformatory labors, Luther had won the respect of a number of young humanists of Germany. Among these were Ulrich von Hutten and Franz von Sickingen. Von Hutten seconded Luther's religious appeals by writing caustic pamphlets against the pope and higher clergy. And von Sickingen, as a close friend, offered his castle to Luther as a place of refuge in case of emergency.

Two other men aided Luther's work and were associated with him at the University of Wittenberg. The first was Andrew Carlstadt, Luther's senior in the divinity school, who had conferred on him the doctor's degree. Carlstadt was an able theologian for those times, but lacked Luther's personality and popular eloquence. He was regarded as somewhat impetuous and often wished to bring about a more complete reformation than did Luther. To Luther's dismay, Carlstadt sometimes *put into practice* what Luther merely talked about.

The other man who became absorbed in Luther's teaching was Philip Melanchthon, the professor of Greek in the university. He was only twenty-one years old at the time, but was scholarly, sensitive, and brilliant—already possessing a wide reputation for his ability. His conversion to Luther's teaching was not because of any travail of spirit, but as a result of his enthusiastic agreement with Luther's interpretation of the writings of Paul.

These humanists, these theologians, the elector, Frederick the Wise, and many other princes, nobles, and scholars—all began to ally themselves with Luther and his teachings. To most of the princes and nobility, the motives were purely *political* and *financial*. They were tired of the domination and intrusion of the Italian papacy. Luther had become a concrete symbol of this long-felt rebellion. Under his leadership, they were united in a *common bond of hatred* against the material power of the Roman Catholic Church (Alzog 202).

To the humanists, Luther became a champion who expressed in popular eloquence what they had written about in witty, erudite books and pamphlets, which were above the understanding of the average man. And his religious appeal gave depth and a positive meaning to the attacks on the hierarchy, which their satirical writings had lacked. Though many did not understand his doctrine of grace, his *spirit of rebellion* against Rome quickly spread.

Thus, Luther became overnight a *champion of all Germany* in their various grievances against the papacy. A real *movement* had now begun, and it was to grow into a conflagration with which neither the pope nor the new emperor, Charles V, could fully cope.

Luther's Doctrinal Development

Luther's treatise entitled, "To the Christian Nobility of the German Nation," issued in 1520, had made him very popular with the German nobility, local authorities, and peasantry. His practical proposals in it are briefly summarized by Walker:

> Papal misgovernment, appointments, and taxation are to be curbed; burdensome offices abolished; German ecclesiastical interests should be placed under a "Primate of Germany"; *clerical marriage* permitted; the far-too-numerous holy days reduced in the interest of industry and sobriety; beggary, including that of the mendicant orders, forbidden; brothels closed; luxury curbed; and theological education in the universities reformed. No wonder the effect of Luther's work was profound. He had voiced what earnest men had long been thinking (Walker, Williston 345).

Later the same year, in his "Babylonian Captivity of the Church," Luther attacked the sacramental practices of the Roman church. He denied the doctrine of transubstantiation, and said there are only two real sacraments—baptism and the Lord's Supper. He denied the scriptural validity of the other Roman sacraments—confirmation, matrimony, orders, and extreme unction—though he did say that penance has a certain sacramental value as a return to the purity of baptism.

In rejecting the unbiblical doctrine of transubstantiation, Luther declared the *absolute authority* of Scripture in matters of faith and practice. He stated, "For that which is asserted without the authority of Scripture or of proven revelation may be held as an opinion, but there is no obligation to believe it... Transubstantiation... must be considered as an invention of human reason, since it is based neither on Scripture nor sound reasoning..." (Bettenson 280).

If Luther had only applied this type of scriptural test to *all* of his doctrines, the world today might be a different type of place! For when he was charged with inserting the word "sola" (*alone*) into Romans 3:28, he haughtily replied, "Should your Pope give himself any useless annoyance about the word *sola*, you may promptly reply: It is the will of Dr. Martin Luther that it should be so" (Alzog 199). And, we may add on good authority, no other reason for such unscriptural changes as these was ever given. When it came to Luther's own personal doctrinal convictions, Martin Luther was truly a *self-willed* man.

The Essence of Luther's Doctrine

To Luther, the essence of the Gospel was *forgiveness of sins* through a personal, transforming faith in Jesus Christ. He regarded this as the *sole type* of true religion (Walker, Williston 346).

But Luther totally neglected the Bible teaching on the kind of absolute *repentance* that must *precede* any forgiveness of sins. And his mind continued to rebel against the necessity of *obedience* to any kind of authority or law after one was forgiven by faith in Christ. He wrote, "As many as *believe* in Christ, be they as numerous and wicked as may be, will be neither responsible for their works nor condemned on account of them." And again: "*Unbelief* is the only sin man can be guilty of; whenever the name is applied to other acts, it is a misnomer..." (Alzog 199).

His third tractate of 1520, "On Christian Liberty," asserts that a Christian man is spiritually *subject to no man nor to any law*. He contended that since we are justified by *faith alone*, we are no longer under obligation to keep the law of God.

Here we see that Luther continued to stress this personal, emotional, and psychological experience of free *forgiveness* as the central tenet of all his teaching. He had himself felt so oppressed by a sense of *guilt* while in the Roman church that he now felt compelled to cast aside all sense of *law* and a need for *obedience*. We will compare this teaching with Scripture in another place.

Thus, Luther's doctrine was now complete in its main outlines. Although he would later clarify himself on many smaller points, the basic principles of Luther's theological system had now been established (Walker, Williston 346).

Luther at Worms and at the Wartburg

In 1521, Luther was summoned to appear before the Diet of Worms, and his friends warned him of his mortal danger. But the emperor had given him a promise of safe conduct, and he was determined to go even "if there were as many devils in that city as there were tiles on its houses."

Appearing before the Diet, Luther was immediately confronted with a row of his books and asked whether he would recant them or not. After a recess for consideration, he admitted that he might have spoken too strongly against persons, but would not recant any of the substance of what he had written, unless it could be disproved by Scripture, or reason. He is reported to have closed with the words: "Here I stand; I can do naught else. God help me. Amen" (Hurlbut 153).

Returning home from Worms, Luther was seized by friendly hands and taken to Wartburg Castle, near Eisenach, where he was to remain in hiding for nearly a year. He had been put under the ban of the empire, and had Germany been ruled by a strong central authority, Luther's career would have soon ended in martyrdom. But his vigorous and friendly territorial ruler, Frederick the Wise, time and again proved to be Luther's salvation. From his secret retreat at the Wartburg, Luther made his continuing activity felt by writing many letters and pamphlets in favor of his cause, which were sent all over Germany. But the most lasting fruit of the period was his translation of the New Testament. This translation from the Greek text of Erasmus into German was a work of high literary value, and is regarded as the foundation of the German written language (Hausser 60–61).

> Few services greater than this translation have ever been rendered to the development of the religious life of a nation. Nor, with all his deference to the Word of God, was Luther without his own canons of criticism. These were the relative clearness with which *his interpretation* of the work of Christ and the method of salvation by faith is taught. Judged by these standards, he felt that Hebrews, James, Jude, and Revelation were of *inferior worth*. Even in Scripture itself there were *differences* in value (Walker, Williston 349).

Thus, we find that although Luther taught that all true doctrine should be based on Scripture, when it came to *interpreting* Scripture he had his own pet theories even as to the relative worth of *entire books* of the Bible! And, as we shall see, he violently denounced those who did not agree with his doctrinal theories.

Continuing Reformation at Wittenberg

While Luther remained in seclusion at Wartburg, several of his associates continued the ecclesiastical revolution in Wittenberg. In many cases they carried out the very reforms that Luther had *talked* about— but had not yet acted on.

By October 1521, Luther's fellow monk, Gabriel Zwilling, was denouncing the mass and urging the abandonment of clerical vows. Many of the inmates of the Augustinian monastery of Wittenberg soon renounced their profession, and Zwilling was soon attacking the use of images.

At Christmas, 1521, Carlstadt summoned the city to a celebration of the Lord's Supper after the *new fashion*. He officiated in plain clothes, omitted all reference to sacrifice in the liturgy, offered *both* the bread and wine to the laity, and used the German language in conducting the sacrament (Bainton 64).

The hearing of confession and the fasts were soon abandoned. Carlstadt taught that all ministers should marry and later, in 1522, took to himself a wife.

The general excitement was increased by the arrival, in December of 1521, of several radical "prophets" from Zwickau. They claimed immediate divine inspiration, taught against infant baptism, and prophesied the speedy end of the world (Walker, Williston 350). Melanchthon was upset by all these events, and was too unsure of himself to affirm or deny these new teachings.

Carlstadt, however, was only trying to follow through on *Luther's appeal* to return to scriptural practices. It is, perhaps, unfortunate that the arrival of the Zwickau "prophets" tainted the movement with radicalism for a time. These incidents were highly displeasing to the elector, Frederick the Wise, and drew forth warning protests from other German princes. It is important to realize that Luther had to walk a narrow line to keep the pleasure of these *German princes* who gave political, military, and financial backing.

And so, partly to avoid any further censure for radicalism from the German princes, and partly because of an evident *jealousy* of *Carlstadt*, Luther was determined to return to Wittenberg and again take charge of the reformatory movement (Orchard 339).

Carlstadt's Reforms

But let us first notice some of the changes Carlstadt was bringing about:

> Carlstadt renounced all clerical garb and, though a minister, dressed in a great gray cloak as a peasant. A second principle re-enforced this position, namely social equalitarianism. The doctrine of the priesthood of all believers was taken so seriously that Carlstadt would not be called Doctor but only "Brother Andreas." The *desire*, which also actuated Luther *to restore the pattern of early Christianity*, was carried farther to include many Old Testament practices. The destruction of images was based on the Mosaic injunction, as was also the introduction of a *strict sabbatarianism*. The *entire program was alien to the spirit of Luther*, who believed that the earth is the Lord's and the fullness thereof, and any portion may be used in the interests of religion (Bainton 65–66).

Upon hearing of this new program, Luther immediately returned to Wittenberg, gained the favor of the Elector and the town council, and *banished* Carlstadt from the city.

The startling fact is here disclosed that Carlstadt, although he *misunderstood some points*, was attempting to reinstate many of the practices of *Christ* and the *Apostles. Luther would have none of this.* He would sometimes *talk* about returning to Biblical Christianity, but he always rejected any real attempt to actually do so.

Luther's Alliance with the Princes

After Luther's return from Wittenberg, he showed a decidedly *conservative attitude* in all things and regained his influence with the German princes. He was forced to *play politics* much of the time because the success of the Lutheran movement was wholly dependent on their favor.

The emperor was now kept busy by a great war with France for the control of Italy. Pope Leo X had died in December 1521, and his successor was not yet influential enough to curb Luther's activities. Under these favorable circumstances, it looked as if the Reformation might win the entire German nation to its cause (Hausser 68–69).

Many Lutheran congregations were now forming in various regions of Germany, and the problem of *church organization* and *government* was presented. Without consulting the *Bible* to find out what type of church government *Christ* had instituted in His Church, Luther thought out *a system of his own.*

> Luther now was convinced that such associations of believers had full power to appoint and depose their pastors. He held, also, however, that the temporal rulers, as in the positions of chief power and responsibility in the Christian community, had a prime duty to further the Gospel. The experiences of the immediate future, and the necessities of actual church organization within extensive territories, were to turn Luther from whatever sympathy he now had with this free-churchism to a strict dependence on the state (Walker, Williston 351).

Because of this very type of *man-devised church government*, we find that the Lutheran Church has been *politically controlled* and almost wholly dependent on the state down to recent times. But Luther's efforts to *keep* the *favor of the German princes*—and his tendency to *retain countless ideas and customs* brought over from the pagan Roman church—all caused him to be considered very "conservative." In fact, he did not depart from the Roman Catholic traditions in *many* ways.

Luther decided that great freedom was permissible in the details of worship, as long as the "Word of God" was kept central. The different Lutheran congregations soon developed a *wide variety* of usages in their services. Instead of Latin, the German language was increasingly used. Luther retained much of the Catholic form of the *Mass*, and issued one in German in 1526. He also retained the Catholic practice of *confession*, though not as obligatory.

> Judged by the development of the Reformation elsewhere, Luther's attitude in manners of worship was strongly conservative, his *principle* being that "what is not contrary to Scripture is for Scripture and Scripture for it." *He therefore retained much of Roman usage*, such as the use of *candles*, the *crucifix*, and the illustrative employment of *pictures* (Walker, Williston 352).

A Rift in Luther's Party

At this time, the first serious rifts among Luther's followers began to appear. The first disaffection arose among the humanists, whose leader, Erasmus, had very little sympathy with Luther's doctrine of "justification by faith *alone*." He feared the results of a teaching that practically *denied the moral responsibility of man*, and the stormy writings of Luther, coupled with tumultuous outbreaks in several places, made him increasingly alarmed.

In the autumn of 1524, he began to challenge Luther's denial of free will. This doctrine, which we will discuss more fully in a later section, asserted that in the fall of Adam, man's nature had become so radically corrupted that he was *incapable of obeying God* or of doing *any* truly good thing.

Realizing the gross error of this doctrine and others held by Luther, and fearful of the increasing decline of interest in education and in public morals, which seemed to accompany Luther's teaching, Erasmus formally broke with Luther (Alzog 226–227).

Another rift in the movement occurred because of the dissatisfaction of some with the halfway measures Luther was taking as a reformer. Many sincerely wanted to get back to the pattern of *New Testament Christianity*. But Luther now seemed determined to preserve as many of the Romish practices and doctrines as he could, without overthrowing his basic doctrines of justification by faith *alone* and rejection of the papal hierarchy and sacramental system. He, no doubt, felt he must do this to keep the *political backing* of the German princes.

It is true that the leaders of some of these movements became *radicals*. An example is Thomas Münzer, who attacked Romanists and Lutherans alike for their doctrines, claiming himself to be *directly inspired*, and leading his followers in ransacking and destroying monasteries and breaking all images in the churches (Walker, Williston 353).

Yet it seems *certain* that if Luther had been willing to trust in God alone for his protection, instead of courting the favor of the human princes, he could have led the people to a *complete break* with the pagan Catholic system, doctrines, and customs. He would have found *many thousands* of sincere men and women in Germany alone who would have *gladly* followed, for the masses were already fed up with the Roman and feudal system and were *ripe* for a change.

Here was a grand opportunity to enact a genuine restoration of the *Christianity of the Apostles*. If Luther and his associates had surrendered their wills completely to God, asked His guidance *in every phase* of this restoration, and honestly followed the plain *literal* word of the *teachings* and *practices* instituted by Christ and His Apostles, much of Germany would probably have followed.

But such was *not* to be the case. Luther's refusal to carry through a complete reformation left many sincere, but uneducated, peasants and townsmen to be the prey of unbalanced leaders, who in many cases restored some of the *truly biblical practices* Luther had willingly ignored—but who, all too often, mingled these with *strange excesses* of their own devising.

The Peasants' War

The situation just described brought on the now-infamous revolt of the German peasants. The way Luther blundered in handling this situation caused by far the most serious separation from his movement.

The German peasantry had been oppressed for generations, and their state was one of increasing misery. The preaching and religious excitement of Luther's reform movement acted as a spark to goad them into the long-delayed action of rising against their masters.

In March 1525, the peasants put forth twelve articles, demanding the right of each community to choose and depose its pastor, that the great tithes (or grain) be used for the support of the pastor and other community expenses, and the small tithes abolished that serfdom be done away, reservations for hunting restricted, the use of the forests allowed to the poor, forced labor be regulated and duly paid, just rents fixed, new laws no longer enacted, common lands restored to communities from which they had been taken, and payments for inheritance to their masters abolished. To modern thinking these were moderate and reasonable requests. To *that age* they seemed revolutionary (Walker, Williston 354).

Although many Protestant historians maintain that Luther had no part in the peasant uprising, it is a *perversion of truth* to deny the fact that the peasants were simply putting into practice some of the principles of freedom *contained in Luther's own writings*. And there is no denying the fact that if Luther had not turned against them in their hour of need, countless thousands of lives would have been spared—and the economic slavery of the German peasantry would not have been prolonged (Hausser 102).

But Luther was suspicious of the uneducated peasant class—in spite of the fact that his own family had belonged to it. And, more importantly, Luther had put his trust in the *backing of the princes*, and was ever careful not to offend them—although he did send them a tempered warning and a reminder of their responsibility in the expected outbreak (Hausser 103).

Luther Advocates Violent Suppression

Because Luther had long advocated the counsel of love and restraint and knew well Christ's injunction to "love your enemies," his about-face in the matter of the peasant revolt is nothing less than astonishing. Furthermore, the situation *did not call for such violence* as he advocated—even had such a course been consistent with Christian principles.

Unquestionably, there were faults on both sides. But Luther's ranting appeal to the princes to *mercilessly destroy* the peasants reveals a spirit as far remote from the Spirit that directed Jesus Christ as it would seem possible to imagine.

Henry C. Vedder paints an accurate picture of the ugly situation:

> Though the peasants had a good cause, they had not always adopted good methods. Most of them were ignorant, all were exasperated, and some were maddened by their wrongs. In their uprising some outrages were committed; castles had been burned and plundered and ruthless oppressors had been slain. These deeds were now made the pretext for a retaliation whose cruelty has rarely been surpassed in history. It is computed by historians, who have no motive to exaggerate, that *fully a hundred thousand were killed* before the fury of the princes and the knights was appeased.
>
> Foremost among those who urged them on was *Luther*. It would seem that he had become alarmed by the persistence of those who had sought to make him and his teachings responsible for the peasant war. *His hope was in the protection and patronage of the princes*, to whom the plain words he had spoken must have given deep offense. So in the midst of the uproar he sent to the press a second pamphlet, in which *he turned completely about*, and denounced the peasants as violently as he had before rebuked the princes.
>
> "They cause uproar, outrageously rob and pillage monasteries and castles not belonging to them. For this alone, as public highwaymen and murderers, *they deserve a twofold death* of body and soul. It is *right* and *lawful to slay* at the first opportunity a rebellious person, known as such, already under God and the emperor's ban. For a public rebel, every man is both judge and executioner. Just as, when a fire starts, he who can extinguish it first is the best fellow. Rebellion is not a vile murder, but like a great fire that kindles and devastates a country; hence uproar carries with it a land full of murder, bloodshed, makes widows and orphans, and destroys

everything, like the greatest calamity. Therefore *whosoever can* should *smite, strangle,* and *stab,* secretly or publicly, and should remember that there is nothing more poisonous, pernicious, and devilish than a rebellious man. Just as when one must slay a mad dog; fight him not and he will fight you, and a whole country with you.

"Let the civil power press on confidently and strike as long as it can move a muscle. For here is the advantage: the peasants have bad consciences and unlawful goods, and *whenever a peasant is killed* therefore *he has lost body* and *soul,* and *goes forever to the devil.* Civil authority, however, has a clean conscience and lawful goods, and can say to God with all security of heart: 'Behold, my God, thou hast appointed me prince or lord, of that I cannot doubt, and has entrusted me with the sword against evil doers (Rom. 13:1-4)... Therefore I will punish and smite as long as I can move a muscle; thou wilt judge and approve.'... *Such wonderful times are these that a prince can more easily win heaven by shedding blood than others with prayer"* (Vedder 173–174).

Well may we ask ourselves, "If these are the words of a reformer sent from God, then *what* is the measure of *true religion*?" Are these the words of a man directed by the Holy Spirit of God? Was the risen Christ using *this* man to purify His "little flock"?

By this cruel act of turning so bitterly against the peasants, Luther had gained greater esteem with the *protecting princes.* But, even humanly speaking, the *cost* was great. From this time forth, popular sympathy for his cause among the peasants of southern Germany was alienated.

Erasmus rebuked Luther for his hypocritical conduct in this sordid affair. He wrote:

We are now gathering the fruits of your teaching. You say indeed that the Word of God should, of its nature, bear very different fruit. Well, in my opinion that greatly depends on the manner in which it is preached. You disclaim any connection with the insurgents, while *they regard you* as their parent, and the author and expounder of their principles (Alzog 223).

After this, it is easy to understand the peasants' lack of sympathy for the man who urged the princes to "*smite, strangle,* and *stab*" them and their loved ones.

The Division of Germany

The bloody suppression of the peasant uprising now left the *princes* and the *cities* in complete control of Germany. Political alliances were now formed for or against the Reformation. A league of Catholics was organized by Duke George of Saxony and other Catholic princes, who met at Dessau in July 1525. An opposing Lutheran league was formed at Torgau. A renewal of the emperor's struggles—this time against an alliance of the pope and the French king—kept Charles V too occupied to interfere with the religious struggles in Germany (Walker, Williston 356).

At the Diet of Spires, in 1526, a decree was made giving each German *prince* the *right to handle religious matters* in his own territory—for the time being—as he felt responsible to God. This act gave the Lutheran movement its first legal existence, and was regarded as a triumph for the German reformers. However, from this time forth Luther was tied to the apron strings of his princely protectors. As we shall see, he was forced to employ *compromise* and *deceit* in order to continue in their good graces. Because of his own system, he was *not allowed* to preach the Word of God "without fear or favor." He and the Protestant cause were inextricably bound up with the *politics* of this world.

But the emperor was soon victorious over all his enemies, and the princes were summoned to the Diet of Spires in 1529. The Catholic party was now in the majority, and issued an edict which forbade the progress of the Reformation in the states which had not accepted it, and granted full liberties in the reformed territories to all who remained Catholics.

To this unequal ruling the Elector of Saxony and several other princes made a formal protest. From that time the term *Protestant* was applied to the Lutheran party and to their doctrines (Fisher, *The History of the Christian Church* 304).

From this time the development of *territorial churches* became an established policy. Germany was to be divided between the Catholic territories in the south and the Protestants in the north.

Now where a man lived often determined his religion. And the spread of Lutheranism depended more on *politics* than on prophets.

Continuing in the next chapter, we will discuss the outcome—the "fruit"—of this religio-political movement. Then we will proceed with the exciting events in other phases of the Reformation. To keep our perspective, we must always bear in mind these questions: Was this movement motivated and guided by God's Holy Spirit? Was it a genuine return to the "faith once for all delivered to the saints"? We will seek the answers to these questions in the next chapter.

Chapter 5

Martin Luther Unleashed

Divisions and scandals plagued the Protestant camp during Luther's later years. The *armies* of princes and *political power* might guarantee that the reformed religion would be outwardly maintained in certain territories. But they had no power to cleanse the faith and morals of subjects, nor were they able to make of one spirit the warring factions that rose *within* the Protestant movement.

During these years began a controversy between the German and Swiss reformers concerning the true meaning of Christ's institution of the Lord's Supper, as it was now called. This contest caused a *lasting breach* between the Lutheran and Reformed Churches—a breach we will examine more fully in a later section.

Meanwhile, in January 1530, the emperor sent a call to the German princes for a Diet to meet in Augsburg. He proposed that the friendly adjustment of religious differences should be the primary object of its meetings.

The Protestants therefore prepared a comprehensive statement of their beliefs and of their criticisms of the Roman Catholic doctrine and practice. It was chiefly drawn up by Luther and Melanchthon, the latter doing most of the actual construction.

The "Augsburg Confession," as it was called, is very important to understand. It is the *official statement* of the position of the Lutheran Church, and has remained the basis of their doctrines to this day.

Let us notice Reginald Walker's scholarly summary of the Lutheran position as set forth by Melanchthon (with Luther's advice) in this creed:

> His *purpose* was to show that the *Lutherans had departed in no vital and essential respect from the Catholic Church*, or even from the Roman Church, as revealed in its earlier writers. That *agreement* is expressly affirmed, and many ancient heresies are carefully repudiated by name. On the other hand, Zwinglian and Anabaptist positions are energetically rejected. The sole authority of Scripture is *nowhere* expressly asserted. The papacy is nowhere categorically condemned. The universal priesthood of believers is not mentioned. Yet Melanchthon gave a thoroughly Protestant tone to the confession as a whole. Justification by faith is admirably defined, the Protestant notes of the church made evident; invocation of saints, the mass, denial of the cup, monastic vows, and prescribed fasting rejected (Walker, Reginald 372).

Protestants Acknowledge Their Unity with the Roman System

Notice first of all that this Confession affirms the *unity* of the Lutherans with the Roman Catholic Church. Stress is given to the fact that Protestant and Catholic are essentially *one church—one system of belief*.

Reference to the sole authority of the Scriptures is by this time *omitted*. The Protestant doctrines of justification by faith *alone* and rejection of the Catholic sacramental system are the *only real points of difference*.

Instead of advocating a return to the *belief* and *faith* and *practice* of Jesus Christ and the true Apostolic Church founded by Him, the reformers now stress the *unity* of Protestantism with the *pagan* philosophies, beliefs, and practices of the *corrupted Roman Catholic system*.

As we have seen, the Romish church had now strayed *as far from the teachings and practices of Christ and the Apostles as would seem possible*. Yet, time and again, we will see the Protestants stressing their "unity" with this reprobate system.

In spite of the conciliatory tone of this Confession, it was rejected by Charles V, and the Catholic-dominated Diet. They ordered the complete restoration of the Catholic faith pending a general council within a year (Hausser 123).

Luther Now Urges War

Fearing punitive measures and the loss of *church property they had seized,* eleven cities united with eight Protestant princes in forming the Schmalkaldic League as a defense against the emperor (Alzog 240–241). It is interesting to note at this juncture that Luther once again *changed his policy for the sake of expediency.*

He had formerly held, with Scripture (Romans 13), that it was a sin to oppose the emperor or any legally constituted authority (Walker, Reginald 375). But now he urged them to employ *violence* to defend his doctrines:

> The Protestant princes, together with certain imperial cities of South Germany, united in the League of Smalcald to resist the arbitrary proceedings of the emperor in his efforts to crush out the new opinions. *Luther,* who had *hitherto opposed a resort to arms,* now declared that Christians were bound to defend their princes when unlawfully assaulted. The league strengthened itself by an alliance with France, Denmark, and the Dukes of Bavaria. The territories of the emperor were again threatened by an irruption of the Turks under Soliman. Under these circumstances, it was impossible to carry out the measures of repression which had been resolved upon at Augsburg. Accordingly, the peace of Nuremberg was concluded in 1532, which provided that religious affairs should be left as they were until they could be arranged by a new diet or a general council" (Fisher, *The History of the Christian Church* 305–306).

From the peace of Nuremberg, the situation of the Protestant territories remained substantially the same for several years. But many enlightening events took place within Luther's camp as the "fruits" of his teaching became more apparent. And in *many* cases, Luther's resort to an *immoral act* as being "expedient" to his cause is to be observed.

Luther Condones Bigamy

Perhaps the most outstanding example of Luther's willingness to *alter his standards* in order to accommodate his princely protectors is the well-known case of Philip I, Landgrave of Hesse. Philip's constant adulteries made him anxious as to his salvation, and he began to reason that perhaps a second marriage to a more attractive wife would be the solution to his problems. He appealed to the Old Testament in an attempt to justify this, with motivation behind his "reasoning" strengthened by his acquaintance with an attractive seventeen-year-old daughter of a lady in his sister's court.

It will be helpful at this point to include extracts from a complete account of this matter by historian Jules Michelet. In it, we find quoted the direct answer of Luther and his associates to the Landgrave's application:

> The most warlike amongst the Protestant chiefs, the impetuous and choleric Landgrave of Hesse, caused it to be represented to Luther, that the *state of his health required him to cohabit with more than one wife*. The instructions given to Bucerus for negotiating this matter with the theologians of Wittemberg offer a curious mixture of sensuality, of religious apprehensions, and of daring frankness.
>
> The application of the Landgrave of Hesse occasioned *extreme embarrassment* to Luther. The whole of the theologians at Wittemberg assembled on the occasion, to frame a reply, in which they determined upon effecting a *compromise* with the prince. *They acceded to his request for permission to take a second wife*, but upon condition that she should not be publicly recognized. "Your highness," they state in their answer, "will, of your own accord, readily suggest to yourself the difference which exists between laying down a law to be universally promulgated, and one to serve a *private and urgent exigency*. We cannot publicly introduce or give our sanction, as by a law, to a permission for marrying a plurality of wives. We implore your highness to reflect upon the danger in which that man would be placed who should be convicted of having introduced into Germany a law such as this, whereby divisions would be instantly created amongst families, and a series of eternal lawsuits arise. Your highness is of a *frail constitution*; you sleep little, and it is requisite to adopt very great *precautions in your case*. The great Scanderbeg frequently exhorted his soldiers to observe chastity, telling them that nothing was so detrimental to their pursuit as the pleasures of love. May it please your highness to examine seriously the various considerations

involved in this matter; the scandal, the labours, the cares, the grief, and weakness, which, as has been shown to you, are involved in it. If, however, your highness is utterly determined upon marrying a second wife, we are of opinion that it ought to be done *secretly*. Signed and sealed at Wittemberg, after the feast of Saint Nicholas, in the year 1539.—Martin Luther, Philip Melancthon, Martin Bucer, Antony Corvin, Adam John Lening, Lustin Wintfert, Dyonisius Melanther" (Michelet 251, 253).

Luther's counsel to make a "secret sin" of this matter was to go unheeded. His *responsibility* for advising the Landgrave to *break God's law* was now to exact its *penalty*. When the news began to leak out, Luther now advised the Landgrave to break *another* of God's *commandments*!

Now Luther Counsels a Lie
"Though an attempt was made to keep the affair private, that soon proved impossible. Luther could only advise 'a good strong lie', but Philip was manly enough to declare: 'I will not lie'" (Walker, Reginald 378).

The scandal resulting from this episode did great damage to the Protestant cause. Thoughtful men were beginning to wonder where Luther's doctrine of "grace *alone*" might lead.

But the main point to remember is that Martin Luther—professing to be a servant of God—had *knowingly* and *deliberately* advocated that a man should *break* two of God's commandments.

In the meantime, the deterioration of morals continued through all classes of Protestant society.

The Protestants had already begun to relax in the severity of their demeanor and practice. They reopened the houses where debaucheries were wont to be carried on. "Better," observed Luther, "would it have been that the devil had never been banished, than that he should return in sevenfold strength" (13 September, 1540) (Michelet 255).

Luther's Death
The course of Protestantism was now firmly in the hands of the *Lutheran princes*, and, with constant threats from the Catholic League, they continued to hold on to the ground gained thus far.

The Catholic Council of Trent opened in 1545. With various interruptions for war, it was to continue to meet in irregular sessions until 1563. Its purpose was mainly to investigate and clear up some of the abuses that had led to the Reformation. The result was a conservative reformation *within* the Catholic Church, but along strictly *Roman* lines, of course.

Soon after this Council began its sessions, and at a time when the emperor had made peace with the Turks and his other enemies, and now seemed ready for a fresh assault against the Protestant princes, Luther made a trip to Eisleben, his birthplace.

In view of the subsequent history of Germany, it will be well to note that Luther's final sermon was a railing attack against the Jewish people. He seems to have been possessed with the same *vicious hatred* and *jealousy* of the Jews as later characterized the rule of Adolph Hitler. Alzog describes this tendency:

> Ascending the pulpit of St. Andrew's Church, in Eisleben, for the last time, Luther once more called down the vengeance of heaven upon the Jews, a race of people whom he had so unjustly and virulently assailed in his earlier writings, that his followers after his death were confused at the very mention of his malignant denunciations. In his first pamphlet against them, he called upon Christians to take the Bible from them, to burn their books and synagogues with pitch and brimstone, and to forbid their worship under penalty of death; and in his second, entitled "Of Shem Hamphoras," he describes them at the very outset as "young devils doomed to hell," who should be driven out of the country (Alzog 271).

Thus, when we read of the atrocities committed against the Jews by Hitler's Third Reich, we may be reminded that such an attitude was remarkably displayed in the founder of German Protestantism.

Luther himself was unhappy and wretched during his last months. Disturbed by the terrible state of morality to which his doctrine of faith *alone* had brought the inhabitants of Wittenberg, he wrote his wife in July, 1545, "Let us go out from this Sodom" (Alzog, p. 270).

It was while prospects were thus darkening that *Luther died* on a visit to Eisleben, the town in which he was born, on February 18, 1546, in consequence of an attack of *heart-disease* or *apoplexy*. His last years had been far from happy. His health had long been wretched. The quarrels of the reformers, to which he had contributed his full share, distressed him. Above all, *the failure* of the pure preaching of justification by faith alone greatly to transform the social, civic, and political life about him grieved him (Walker, Reginald 379).

Thus, it was even apparent to Luther that his doctrines had in large measure *failed to cause men to lead lives more consistent with spiritual principles*. He often had periods of despondency in his last years, when he seriously wondered if he were not dragging many souls with him to eternal condemnation (Plummer 132).

After Luther's death, the Protestant princes suffered a military defeat at the battle of Muhlberg, in 1547. The emperor granted an *interim*, which was essentially a victory for the Catholics, until another session of the Council of Trent could be called.

The Reformation Settlement

But in 1554, the Lutheran prince Maurice of Saxony united with Henry II of France to inflict a crushing defeat on Charles V. The Lutherans now demanded full religious freedom and the right to keep *all ecclesiastical property seized thus far* (Alzog 279–280).

A compromise called the Peace of Augsburg was finally reached in September 1555. It permitted each prince to determine whether Catholicism or Lutheranism should be professed in his territory. *No choice* was given his subjects. All ecclesiastical properties seized before 1552 were to be retained by the Lutherans; all seizures since that time were to be returned. *Only* Catholicism and Lutheranism (as defined in the Augsburg Confession) were permitted in Germany. All other deviationists were to continue to be punished as "heretics" (Walker, Reginald 382).

Therefore, in 1555, the division of Germany between Catholic and Lutheran was made permanent. In after years, the most serious challenge to this state of things was made in the Thirty Years' War (1618–1648). In the course of this terrible war, between the princes of the *Catholic League* and those of the *Protestant Union*, nearly *half* the population of Germany is said to have perished by the sword, famine, or the plague. But, by the Peace of Westphalia, it finally ended in relatively the same religious division of Germany as had been decided upon in the Peace of Augsburg.

Thus, religious hatred, political division, and unceasing war continued to follow in the wake of the Lutheran reform. The decline in public morals was also a noticeable factor, as we shall see.

The *political* and *religious alliance* of Luther *with the German princes* placed the destiny of his cause in their hands from the first. And this religious patriotism, in turn, prepared the way for the *strong national state* in Germany.

Before analyzing the doctrines and practices of the Lutheran movement and the ultimate *result* of this religious upheaval, we will first recount the course of the Reformation in other lands, such as Switzerland, France, and England.

And lest we lose our *perspective* in the maze of historical events, places, and personalities, let us again ask ourselves: Was the Protestant Reformation a movement *activated* of original, first-century Christianity? Were its "fruits" the result of the Holy Spirit's operation? Was the Protestant movement a genuine "reformation" of the one true Church which Jesus promised to build? (Matthew 16:18). Was it a sincere, Spirit-led return to the "faith which was once for all delivered to the saints?" (Jude 3).

Now we shall continue this revealing analysis of the Reformation with the dramatic story of its progress in Switzerland. We shall first consider the man who began the reform movement in that land. He is little known to most modern churchgoers, yet he has exerted a powerful influence on the beliefs and practices many Protestant churches hold to this day. His name was Ulrich Zwingli.

The Zwinglian Reform

During the early years of the Lutheran reform, a movement that was similar in many respects began in Switzerland. The guiding force of this movement in its early stages was *Ulrich Zwingli.*

Zwingli was born in 1484 in the mountain village of Wildhaus and was a bright student from his youth. He studied at the University of Vienna and then went to Basel. He became absorbed in humanism, and later began studying the Greek Testament published by Erasmus. From this, he copied with his own hand the epistles of Paul that he might commit them to memory.

In addition to his scholarly interests, Zwingli was also a *zealous patriot* and wished to reform the corrupt *social* and *political life* of his country. Bribes and ecclesiastical positions were commonly offered influential Swiss to gain their allegiance in fighting the battles of the pope or of the French king (Hausser 127–128).

After receiving his master's degree at the University of Basel, Zwingli was appointed as a parish priest through the influence of his uncle. He himself received for a time a pension from the pope by consenting to the hiring of Swiss youths as mercenary soldiers in the pope's army (Walker, Reginald 360).

He was finally led to denounce this practice of mercenary hiring because of vigorous French activities to this end in his own parish. Zwingli then was able to effect a transfer of his activities to the famous pilgrim shrine of Einsiedeln, which greatly enlarged his influence and reputation.

Zwingli's Doctrinal Development

During this time, Zwingli was led to see the futility of the superstitious pilgrimages made each year to the religious shrines in Einsiedeln, and was led to preach against one Samson, a seller of *indulgences.*

He also continued at this time his study of Scripture and began to develop a *doctrine of justification* similar to Luther's. He remembered some of the humanist lectures he had heard in the university, exposing the worthlessness of indulgences and affirming the death of Christ as the only price of forgiveness. He began to feel that Scripture was the only authority and, through its study, developed many points that came out in his later teaching.

In 1518, Zwingli was transferred to the cathedral church of Zurich. He now refused his papal pension, and opposed all foreign entanglements of the Swiss. It was not until 1522 that Zwingli definitely *broke with Rome.*

When some of his parishioners broke the Lenten fast, citing Zwingli's doctrine of the sole authority of the Scriptures (Hausser 132), he preached and published in their defense, and the bishop of Constance sent a commission to put down the innovations. Zwingli now appealed to the *civil authorities,* and the Zurich burgomaster eventually ruled that only those things taught in Scripture were to be preached. Thus, the road was open for a *religious* and *political* revolution.

Rapid Changes Occur

News of the Reformation in Germany under Luther had now reached most of Switzerland, and this was an additional encouragement to their cause. Many of Luther's writings were also being distributed among the German-speaking Swiss, and his doctrine of *justification by faith alone* was now widely understood (Fisher, *The Reformation* 147).

But, as we shall see, with the aid of the *civil authorities,* who were fed up with Roman tyranny, Zwingli was able to bring about an even *greater change* than had Luther.

Zwingli believed that the *ultimate authority* was the Christian community, and that the exercise of that authority was through the duly constituted organs of *civil government* acting in accordance with the Scriptures. Only that which the Bible commands, or for which distinct authorization can be found in its pages, is binding or allowable (Walker, Reginald 361).

Because of his strong belief that the Bible ought to be the *complete guide* in doctrine and practice, Zwingli went much farther than Luther in his reform. His attitude toward the heathen ceremonies and feasts that had crept into the Roman Catholic Church was much stricter than that of Luther. "While Luther was disposed to leave untouched what the Bible did not prohibit, Zwingli was more inclined to reject what the Bible did not enjoin" (Fisher, *The Reformation*, 145).

Zwingli now began the process of getting cantonal government officials to back his teaching. He arranged for a public debate on sixty-seven articles, involving the Catholic doctrines on the mass, good works, intercession of saints, monastic vows, and the existence of purgatory. The *Bible* was to be the authority on which the discussion was to be based. "In the resulting debate the government declared Zwingli the victor, in that it affirmed that he had not been convicted of heresy, and directed that he should continue his preaching. It was an endorsement of his teaching" (Walker, Reginald 362).

Many changes now took place. The priests and nuns began to marry. Images, relics, and organs were done away. The *confiscation of ecclesiastical properties* by the state began in 1524. That same year, Zwingli married a woman with whom he had lived since 1522—not without *considerable scandal* (Walker, Reginald 363).

Because of the political value of Switzerland in the wars, the pope had not directly interfered with the Zwinglian movement all this time. Zwingli encouraged the spread of his movement throughout Switzerland. Most of the cities soon came under the influence of his teaching, and even the great German city of Strasbourg had been won to the Zwinglian, rather than the Lutheran, point of view.

It is important to note, however, that the changes were *not* actually accompanied by the wholesale conversion of the individuals in these cities to Zwingli's teachings. Rather, it was a combination *politico-religious movement* aided by the Swiss Republican Party, which came to oppose *all things Roman*. It was this very alliance with *politics* that soon led to Zwingli's death on the battlefield.

Zwingli's Basic Doctrinal Position

In 1525, Zwingli published his main theological work, the "Commentary on True and False Religion." Fisher summarizes his doctrinal position:

> Although in *most points* he held the *ordinary Protestant views*, he differed from them in the doctrine of the Sacrament, as will hereafter be explained. He held to predestination as a philosophical tenet, but taught that Christ has redeemed the entire race. He considered original sin a disorder rather than a state involving guilt. He believed that the sages of antiquity were illuminated by the Divine Spirit, and in his catalogue of saints he placed Socrates, Seneca, the Catos, and even Hercules (Fisher, *The History of the Christian Church* 308).

Here we note that Zwingli so *totally misunderstood* the purpose and nature of God's Holy Spirit as to imagine that it was guiding the *pagan* philosophers of antiquity, whose *immoral lives* and *teachings* are clearly alluded to by the Apostle Paul in his letter to Christians in Rome (Romans 1:18–32).

Of course, many Protestant writers acclaim Zwingli for his "broad" views on the heathen speculators. Hastie lauds Zwingli's view: "With a breadth of thought and feeling rare in his age, he recognized a *divine inspiration* in the thoughts and lives of the *nobler spirits of antiquity*, such as Socrates, Plato, and Seneca, and hoped even to meet with them *in heaven*" (Hastie 184).

Zwingli's desire to meet these ancient philosophers in heaven is illuminating to the real student of Scripture. He had altered many outward

Catholic forms for the better, and had adopted Luther's fundamental doctrine of justification, but his *entire concept* of God and of the ultimate *purpose* of salvation was still essentially that of the Roman Catholic Church.

The Lutheran and Zwinglian branches of the Protestant movement had scarcely begun to develop when they came into a violent controversy on the doctrine of the Lord's Supper, as they called it. It was a basic matter for both parties, and neither would give ground or yield to the other.

The Controversy Over the Lord's Supper

Though Luther had rejected the unbiblical doctrine of transubstantiation, he insisted that the objective, real presence of the glorified body and blood of Christ was actually *in* the bread and wine—a condition he called "sacramental union." He denied that the bread and wine were somehow "changed" into Christ's actual body and blood. Yet, he still argued that, in some mysterious way, Christ's body and blood are actually received by the communicant during the Eucharist ceremony.

On the other hand, Zwingli denied that the body or blood of Christ is actually present in any such sense, and believed the Lord's Supper to be simply a *memorial* of His atoning death.

In the dispute, little love was shown on either side. Zwingli thought that Luther's idea of the *real* presence of Christ in the Eucharist was a continuing form of *Catholic superstition*. He said that a physical body could only be in *one place*, and that Christ was at the right hand of the Father in heaven.

Luther accused Zwingli of exalting human reason above Scripture. He tried to explain the physical presence of Christ on ten thousand altars at once to be a scholastic assertion that the qualities of Christ's divine nature were not communicated to His human nature and so, as spirit, He could be *everywhere at once*.

Perhaps the significant thing is that this dispute showed clearly that—*whether either one was right*—they were *not of the same spirit*. From then on, they *could not honestly claim* that the *one* Holy Spirit of God was guiding them into truth—and that they were one in Christian fellowship.

Luther declared Zwingli and his supporters to be *no Christians*, while Zwingli affirmed that Luther was *worse* than the Roman champion, Eck. Zwingli's views, however, met the approval not only of German-speaking Switzerland, but, of much of south-western Germany. The Roman party rejoiced at this evident *division* of the Evangelical forces (Walker, Reginald 364).

The heated controversy over this point extended for many years, and included a series of pamphlets, preachments, and discussions. The principal and, as far as results, final discussion between the reformers on this point took place in the castle of Philip I, the Landgrave of Hesse mentioned earlier in this chapter, in Marburg.

It should seem peculiar that an *adulterer*, a *bigamist*, and a *drunkard* like the Landgrave should be one of the lay leaders in the Reformation movement.

But Philip was one of the *political mainstays* of the Protestant movement, and desired that the two reforming parties come to an agreement, if at all possible. Therefore, he invited the leaders of both parties to meet at his castle and on October 1, 1529, the discussions began.

Although Luther was suspicious of the doctrine of the Swiss on the *trinity* and the *original sin*, the main point of difference was the presence or absence of Christ's *physical* body in the Lord's Supper. Luther insisted on a literal interpretation of the words: "This is my body." Zwingli held that a *physical body* could not be in *two places* at one time. Though the discussions lasted for several days, agreement was impossible, and the two parties finally parted—each doubting the "Christianity" of the other (Kurtz 273).

The Landgrave arranged one final meeting of the reformers, and urged upon them the importance of coming to some sort of understanding.

The Final Meeting of Luther and Zwingli
Schaff describes this meeting:

On Monday morning he arranged another private conference between the Saxon and the Swiss Reformers. They met for the last time on earth. With tears in his eyes, Zwingli approached Luther, and held out the hand of *brotherhood*: but *Luther declined it*, saying again, "Yours is a *different spirit* from ours." Zwingli thought that differences in non-essentials, with unity in essentials, did not forbid Christian brotherhood. "Let us," he said, "confess our union in all things in which we agree; and, as for the rest, let us remember that we are brethren. There will never be peace in the churches if we cannot bear differences on secondary points." Luther deemed the corporal presence a fundamental article, and construed Zwingli's liberality into indifference to truth. "I am astonished," he said, "that you wish to consider me as your brother. It shows clearly that you do not attach much importance to your doctrine." Melanchthon looked upon the request of the Swiss as a strange inconsistency. Turning to the Swiss, the Wittenbergers said, "You do not belong to the communion of the Christian Church. *We cannot acknowledge you as brethren.*" They were willing, however, to include them in that universal charity which we owe to our enemies (Schaff 7: 644–645).

Thus, we see that Luther parted from Zwingli, *not* in the feeling that the Swiss party was guided by the Holy Spirit, but that Zwingli was guided by a *different* "spirit" than himself. Indeed, there is ample testimony, even among Protestant writers, that the reformers did *not* have the "unity of the Spirit" that only *God's* Spirit can bring.

Notice Plummer's account of Zwingli's desire to avoid this pathetic disagreement:

But, there is no need to doubt his declaration that he had carefully avoided corresponding with Luther, because he says, "I desired to show to all men the uniformity of the Spirit of God, as manifested in the fact that we, who are so far apart, are in unison one with the other, yet without collusion." They did *not remain in unison*, as all the world knows; and it is one of the many sad facts in the history of the Reformation that Luther declared Zwingli's violent death to be a *judgment* on him for his eucharistic doctrine (Plummer 141–142).

Zwingli's Death

Soon after the Marburg Conference, a war broke out between the cantons of Switzerland, which resulted in the death of Zwingli. It began as a direct result of the attempt of the Protestant cities to starve the Catholic cantons into submission, and ended with the Catholics repossessing some of the ground they had previously lost.

The trouble developed out of the persecution of the Protestants in the Catholic cantons. The behavior of the Catholic cantons became threatening, and Zwingli recommended a resort to *violent measures* to force them into submission.

> The chief demands that were really made were that the Protestant doctrine, which was professed in the lower cantons, should be tolerated in the upper, and that persecution should cease there. But the question was whether even these demands would be enforced. *Zwingli* was in favor of overpowering the enemy by a *direct attack*, and of *extorting* from them just concessions. But he was overruled, and half measures were resorted to. The attempt was made to coerce the Catholic cantons by nonintercourse, by thus *cutting off their supplies*. The effect was the Catholics were enabled to collect their strength, while the Protestant cities were divided by jealousies and by disagreement as to what might be the best policy to adopt. Zurich was left without help, to confront, with hasty and inadequate preparation, the combined strength of the Catholic party. The Zurich force was defeated at Cappel, on the 11th of October, 1531, and Zwingli, who had gone forth as a chaplain with his people to battle, fell (Fisher, *The Reformation* 153–156).

Why Zwingli Died in Battle

The cruel truth is that Zwingli's violent death was a *direct result* of his own actions. He had *not heeded* the biblical injunction to "keep [himself] unspotted from the world" (James 1:27). *Neglecting* to apply Christ's declaration: "My kingdom is *not of this world*" (John 18:36), Zwingli had made constant use of *politics* and physical *power* to gain the results he desired.

As Fisher states: "Zwingli was a *patriot* and a *social reformer*" (Fisher, *The Reformation* 145). Like Luther, he put his trust in the princes of *this world*.

Therefore, Zwingli's violent death on the battlefield—in an essentially *religious* war which he himself had urged—seems a striking confirmation of Christ's warning: "For all who take the sword will *perish* by the sword" (Matthew 26:52).

After his death, the reformed party could still have gained the victory. But it was *not united*, and each city aspired to be the metropolis of a proposed confederation—and so was *jealous* of the others. Consequently, they were forced to conclude a humiliating peace, and had to yield some of the gains they had previously made (Kurtz 269).

Thus, we see *division* among Zwingli's followers, and an even *greater division* between them and the Lutherans. That same spirit of *mutual antagonism* possessed many of their Protestant successors in the generations that followed.

One has only to look about him to see the hundreds of *differing* Protestant churches. On occasion, for a show of unity, they call themselves, collectively, the "Church of Christ." But they are *not* of one spirit by any means.

At the very beginning of this division among the Protestant churches, Martin Luther was willing to *face this fact*. Referring to Zwingli and his followers, he said: "Either one party or the other must *necessarily* be working in the service of Satan; the matter does not admit of discussion, there is *no possibility of compromise*" (Alzog 352).

Thus began the religious *division* and *confusion* of our times. Our *purpose* is to determine if this Protestant system—or *any part of it*—is a genuine restoration of the *one* true Church Jesus Christ said He would build. In the next chapter, we will continue with the study of John Calvin's tremendous influence on the Reformation. You will be *surprised* to find out the truth about the origin of many modern Protestant ideas!

Chapter 6

The Birth of Calvinism

In the last chapter, we began the story of the Swiss reformation, and saw the part that Ulrich Zwingli played in it. As was the case with the other reformers, we were forced to observe that Zwingli's example was also in striking contrast to the teaching and example of Christ and the early apostles. Zwingli's violent death in a war he himself had urged certainly confirms Jesus' warning, "all who take the sword will perish by the sword" (Matthew 26:52).

Often, we have paused to ask: Was the Protestant movement a reformation of God's true Church gone wrong? Was this movement inspired and guided by God's Holy Spirit?

Now we will come to the story of the man who really dominated the Swiss reformation—and has dominated much of Protestantism since.

The Reformation Under John Calvin

John Calvin now enters the Reformation drama, and we will see that the powerful influence of his mind and personality will dramatically shape the doctrinal system of the reformed congregations for generations to come (Kurtz 304–305). Like Luther and Zwingli before him, Calvin was trained for the Catholic priesthood. Thus, he too, had deeply ingrained in his mind many concepts imparted by the Roman Church, although his doctrinal break with the papacy was more complete than Luther's had been.

It is nevertheless significant that the three most prominent leaders among the early reformers were all trained as "Roman" theologians before beginning their reformatory activities. Perhaps this may explain, in part, why they all retained many pagan concepts and traditions that had crept into the Roman system during the Dark Ages.

While Zwingli was busy transforming the religious and political life of Switzerland, John Calvin was still a youth—training for the Catholic priesthood.

Calvin was a Frenchman, and he was born in the year 1509 at Noyon, in Picardy. His father was a fiscal agent, and Calvin was educated with children of noble birth. At just twelve years of age, he was appointed to a chaplaincy with an income sufficient for his support.

Soon after, he was sent to Paris to study for the priesthood, but his father later changed his plans and wished Calvin to become a lawyer. He then went to Orleans and Bourges, and studied under celebrated doctors of the law. He was such a brilliant scholar that he was often invited to take over in a professor's absence.

At this time, he came under the influence of a relative, Peter Olivetan, who was the first Protestant to translate the Bible into French. By studying the New Testament in the original Greek, Calvin further strengthened his interest in the Protestant doctrines.

Not long after publishing a learned humanistic treatise on the writings of Seneca, his "sudden conversion"—as he later described it—took place. He now desired to throw himself upon the mercy of God, and began an earnest study of the Bible (Fisher, *The History of the Christian Church* 319).

Calvin returned to Paris and soon became a recognized leader of the Protestants there. Persecution drove him out of the city, and Calvin eventually settled temporarily in Protestant Basel.

It was at this time that the French monarch, Francis I, was trying to get the aid of the German Lutheran princes against the emperor, Charles V. In order to justify his persecutions of French Protestants, he accused them of all the lawless fanaticism of some of the extreme Anabaptist sects.

This called forth from Calvin an elaborate defense of his French fellow believers. This work was intended to prove the falsity of Francis I's charges, and to set forth the Protestant beliefs in a systematic and logical way that might win sympathy from the king and others for the reformers' cause (Kurtz 302).

Calvin's *Institutes*

This work was entitled, *Institutes of the Christian Religion*. It was regarded as a tremendous contribution to *theology*, and to *literature* as well. No French Protestant had yet spoken with such logic and power. This work is still regarded as the most orderly and systematic presentation of doctrine and of the Christian life that the Reformation produced (Walker, Williston 392).

To briefly comprehend Calvin's doctrine as contained in the *Institutes*, we can do no better than to quote excerpts from Walker's summary of the position Calvin took in this work:

> Without Luther's antecedent labors, his work could not have been done. It is *Luther's* conception of *justification by faith*, and of the sacraments as seals of God's promises that he presents. Much he derived from Butzer, notably his emphasis on the glory of God as that for which all things are created, on *election* as a doctrine of Christian confidence, and on the consequences of election as a strenuous endeavor after a life of conformity to the will of God. But all is systematized and clarified with a skill that was Calvin's own.

> Man's highest knowledge, Calvin taught, is that of God and of himself. Enough comes by nature to leave man without excuse, but adequate knowledge is given only in the Scriptures, which the witness of the Spirit in the heart of the believing reader attests as the very voice of God. The Scriptures teach that God is good, and the source of all goodness everywhere. *Obedience* to God's will is man's primal duty. As originally created, man was good and capable of obeying God's will, but he lost goodness and power alike in Adam's fall, and is now, of himself, *absolutely incapable* of goodness. Hence *no work* of man's can have any merit; and all men are in a state of ruin meriting only damnation. From this helpless and hopeless condition some men are undeservedly rescued through the work of Christ.

> Since all good is of God, and *man is unable to initiate or resist his conversion*, it follows that the reason some are saved and others are lost is the *divine choice*—election and reprobation. For a reason for that choice beyond the will of God it is absurd to inquire, since God's will is an ultimate fact.

Three institutions have been divinely established by which the Christian life is maintained—the *church*, the *sacraments*, and *civil government*. In the last analysis the church consists of "all the elect of God"; but it also properly denotes "the whole body of mankind... who profess to worship one God and Christ." Yet there is no true church "where lying and falsehood have usurped the ascendancy" (Walker, Williston 392–394).

Calvin's Doctrinal Position Examined

We can see that Calvin's doctrine of justification by faith *alone* came from Luther. Yet Calvin did believe that a "saved" person is to produce *good works* as necessary fruit of his conversion.

Calvin emphasized man's responsibility to follow the *law of God* as a guide to the Christian life (Walker, Williston 393). However, in *no sense* did he mean this to include the letter of the Ten Commandments, but only the "spirit" of God's moral law as it came to be defined by *Calvin*. In actual practice, as we shall see, there were *many times* when this led men to *break* both the letter and the spirit of the literal Ten Commandments. We shall cite examples of this later.

Without question, the *foundational principle* of Calvin's entire theological system is his *doctrine of predestination*. In it, all other things were made to conform to the irrevocable will of God. As did Luther, Calvin derived many of his ideas on this subject from Augustine (Fisher, *The History of The Christian Church* 321).

In the section on predestination in his *Institutes of the Christian Religion,* Calvin dogmatically states:

> No one who wishes to be thought religious dares outright to deny *predestination*, by which God chooses some for the hope of life, and condemns others to eternal death.... By predestination we mean the eternal decree of God, by which he has decided in his own mind what he wishes to happen in the case of each individual. For *all men are not created on an equal footing,* but *for some eternal life is preordained, for others eternal damnation...* (Bettenson 302).

As the Protestant historians themselves tell us, *this* is the essence of Calvinism!

Let us consider the *meaning* of these dogmatic assertions. First, Calvin says that all men are *not created equal* before God. But the Apostles Peter and Paul were both inspired to write: "God is *no respecter* of persons" (Acts 10:34; Romans 2:11, *King James Version*).

Next, Calvin tells us that—*regardless of what they may do*—some men are absolutely *predetermined* for eternal *life*, others for eternal *damnation*.

Calvin's Idea of Predestination

Thus, we find that the terrifying proposition that men are *born* to be "saved" or "lost" was one of the basic tenets of Calvin's doctrine. According to this theory, you are predestined from *all eternity* to either the *joys* of heaven, or the *torments* of a burning hell. Of your own will, you are *not able to repent* and be *converted*. This is *only* possible for those whom God has "elected" to grace.

As we have seen, Calvin also taught that once a person has been forgiven and justified through Christ, he can *never* fall away. Viewing this practically, it means that no matter how *wicked* a "saved" person might become, no matter how utterly *depraved, blasphemous,* and *reprobate* he might be at the end of his days, he is nevertheless foreordained and bound to inherit the unspeakable delights of heaven through *all eternity*. Those predestined to be "lost" are doomed—as the "reformed" preachers would put it—to an eternity in the *burning, screaming, horrifying tortures of a never-ending hell.*

Such was the doctrine of John Calvin. And this became the teaching of the "reformed" congregations as they later spread throughout parts of France, into Scotland, to other nations of Europe, and finally—through the "Puritans"—to the New England states.

Calvin at Geneva

Shortly after publishing his *Institutes,* Calvin visited Italy for a brief time. On his way back to Basel, he had to pass through Geneva. An event occurred there that changed the course of his life.

In 1532, after the Protestant defeat at the battle of Cappel, a reforming preacher named William Farel had come to Geneva to revive the Protestant forces in their city. Like Calvin, he had been driven out of France by Catholic persecution. Because of his powerful and unrestrained preaching, he had at first been expelled from Geneva. But he later returned, and led the Protestants to gain complete control of this city.

Because all "worldly" pleasures and entertainment were banned by his religious party, a great deal of strife had arisen and the city was in turmoil. Farel, therefore, knowing the great ability of Calvin and his interest in the Protestant cause, persuaded him to stay and help the reformed party control the city. Calvin at first had preferred the quiet seclusion of the scholarly life, but finally yielded when Farel warned that "God's curse" would fall on him if he refused to help.

Calvin then set to work immediately. He composed a catechism for the instruction of the young, and aided in formulating a stringent set of laws that forbade the people to wear "vain" ornaments or participate in "obnoxious" sports and other worldly amusements (Fisher, *The History of the Christian Church* 324).

But the Libertines, as the opposing party was called, soon gained the upper hand and *banished* Calvin and Farel from the city.

This was 1538, and Calvin went to Strasbourg, where he spent most of his three years' absence from Geneva. He took charge of a Protestant church for French refugees there, and soon took a wife. It was here also that he formed a personal acquaintance with Philip Melanchthon, who gradually came over to his view of the Lord's Supper, though the two never agreed on predestination.

He was now recalled to Geneva to help the triumphant reformed party found a *political* and *ecclesiastical government* upon the principles of their belief. From here on we notice Calvin's increasing involvement in *politics* and resulting *religious strife* (Walker, Williston 397–398).

Calvin's Return to Geneva

Calvin returned victorious to Geneva in 1541, and set up a new *political* and *ecclesiastical* order. It was surprisingly similar to the Catholic church-state relationship of obedient nations within the Holy Roman Empire.

The state was *dominated* by the religious leaders, and was bound to foster the interests of the church, carry out its orders, and to *punish* or *execute* all those who opposed the established religion. Calvin had never rid himself of the Catholic concept of the *church ruling the state* and mixing in worldly politics.

Not only profaneness and drunkenness, but innocent amusements and the teaching of divergent theological doctrines,
were *severely punished*. Nor was this all. Trifling offenses
were visited with severe penalties. It was impossible that
a city of twenty thousand inhabitants should rest content
under such stringent discipline and such stern enactments.
The elements of disaffection disclosed themselves soon after
Calvin's return. His chief opponents, as before, were the
Libertines (Fisher, *The History of the Church* 325).

Calvin tried to enforce this kind of *dogmatic system* on the entire
city from this time until his death. Naturally, it could lead to nothing
but *trouble*, and the chronicle of Calvin's later life is mainly concerned
with his problems in trying to *suppress* the city of Geneva and *coerce*
its inhabitants into yielding to his views. There is no denying the fact
that he was a kind of *religious dictator!*

The Calvinistic Discipline

Beyond noting the famous case of Michael Servetus, which will be
covered in a later chapter, a detailed explanation of the *cruelty* and
rigor with which Calvin *enforced* his system of belief on the hapless
Genevans is unnecessary. The only thing that needs to be said is that
the "fruits" of Calvin's teaching at Geneva make a striking *contrast*
to the inspired statement of Paul: "… For the kingdom of God is not
eating and drinking, but righteousness and peace and joy in the Holy
Spirit" (Romans 14:17).

The following summary of the effect of Calvin's "Theocracy" on
Geneva should provide ample basis for comparison:

Let us give a summary of the most striking cases of discipline. Several women, among them the wife of Ami
Perrin, the captain-general, were *imprisoned for dancing*
(which was usually connected with excesses). Bonivard,
the hero of political liberty, and a friend of Calvin, was
cited before the Consistory because he had played at dice
with Clement Marot, the poet, for a quart of wine. A man
was *banished* from the city for three months because, on
hearing an ass bray, he said jestingly: "He prays a beau-

tiful psalm." A young man was *punished* because he gave his bride a book on housekeeping with the remark: "This is the best Psalter." A lady of Ferrara was expelled from the city for expressing sympathy with the Libertines, and abusing Calvin and the Consistory. Three men who had laughed during the sermon were *imprisoned* for three days. Another had to do public penance for neglecting to commune on Whitsunday. Three children were punished because they remained outside of the church during the sermon to eat cakes... A person named Chapuis was *imprisoned* for four days because he persisted in calling his child Claude (a Roman Catholic saint) instead of Abraham, as the minister wished, and saying that he would sooner keep his son unbaptized for fifteen years. Bolsec, Gentilis, and Castellio were *expelled* from the Republic for heretical opinions. Men and women were *burnt* for witchcraft. Gruet was *beheaded* for sedition and atheism. Servetus was *burnt* for heresy and blasphemy. The last is the most flagrant case which, more than all others combined, has exposed the name of Calvin to abuse and execration; but it should be remembered that he wished to substitute the milder punishment of the sword for the stake, and in this point at least he was in advance of the public opinion and usual practice of his age (Schaff, 490–492).

Schaff's plea that Calvin's "mercy" was in advance of his age sounds somewhat hollow when we remember that he and the other reformers *condemned* the papacy for the same brutalities and referred to Christ's example of love by way of contrast.

Perhaps we need to remind ourselves that Jesus taught Christians in His age, "Judge not, that you be not judged" (Matthew 7:1). And again, "But if you do not forgive men their trespasses, neither will your Father forgive your trespasses" (Matthew 6:15).

This teaching certainly is in contrast with Calvin's "theocracy" in Geneva. We continue Schaff's description of that frightful system:

The official acts of the Council from 1541 to 1559 exhibit a dark chapter of censures, fines, imprisonments, and executions. During the ravages of the pestilence in 1545 more than *twenty men and women were burnt alive* for witchcraft, and a wicked conspiracy to spread the horrible disease. From 1542 to 1546 fifty-eight judgments of death and seventy-six decrees of banishments were passed. During the years 1558 and 1559 the cases of various punishments for all sorts of offenses amounted to four hundred and fourteen—a very large proportion for a population of 20,000 (Schaff 492).

Thus, we see that Calvin was willing not only to *punish*, but to *execute* those who failed to go along with his theological system. Two years after the burning of Servetus, the Libertine party in Geneva made a last determined effort to overthrow the religious hierarchy that Calvin had set up. They first attempted intrigue and secret diplomacy, but finally resorted to armed conflict in May of 1555.

But Calvin's forces were the stronger, and this last rebellion was a death blow to the Libertine party. Many now had to flee for their lives from the "justice" of Calvin (Walker, Williston 400).

At this point, we should take note of the fact—as evidenced by the foregoing examples of Calvin's system—that he was the primary reformer who stressed the idea that men are to *forsake all pleasure* in this life.

Therefore, as we have seen, such trifling things as card-playing, dancing, jesting and theatre-going were treated as *major sins*. In many cases, Geneva's religious courts would punish such an offender with *public whipping* or even possibly *death!*

These harsh measures were the result of the concept that God is a stern, unrelenting Judge who wishes all men to *suffer*. He frowns upon any of the common pleasures of man. Most pleasing to Him, taught Calvin, is a life of *barrenness, poverty* and *severity*.

Perhaps without realizing it, thousands of Protestants to this day have been influenced by this concept and have a *feeling of guilt* even regarding many of the innocent pleasures of life. The strict "blue laws" of the New England Puritans are an example of this, and the same tendency is evident to this day among many of the stricter Protestant sects.

It is well to realize that this teaching did not come from the Bible. For the most part, it came from *John Calvin's rigid mind.*

Calvin's Last Days

The Libertine rebellion having been crushed, Calvin was the undisputed master of Geneva. In 1559, he founded the "Geneva Academy"—later to be known as the University of Geneva. It soon became the greatest center of theological instruction in the Reformed communities, as distinguished from the Lutheran.

Those in all nations who were struggling to advance the cause of *Reformed Protestantism looked to Geneva* for instruction and support. It became the great seminary from which ministers went forth to France, the Netherlands, England, Scotland, Germany, and Italy. Almost as an *absolute ruler* of Geneva, Calvin, as Hausser comments, "acquired and maintained more power than was ever exercised by the most powerful popes" (Hausser 250).

To the end, Calvin labored diligently in preaching and writing. He came to look upon the spread of the *Protestant Churches* over the world as being synonymous with the coming of the *Kingdom of God.*

Here is one of the most significant differences between Calvin and the previous reformers. He rejected their expectation of the speedy coming of the Lord and projected the final cataclysm into an *indefinite future.* Luther looked wistfully for the end of the age before his own demise and the Anabaptists often set dates. But Calvin renewed the role of St. Augustine who terminated the early Christian expectation of the speedy coming of the Lord, and envisaged successive acts in the historical drama in which *the Church came well-nigh to be equated with the Kingdom of God.* Even so Calvin substituted for the great and imminent day of the Lord the dream of the Holy Commonwealth in the terrestrial sphere. Its erection depended upon *human agents*, God's chosen instruments, the elect (Bainton 114).

This attitude caused men to become so absorbed in what we today must sadly speak of as "churchianity" that they *failed to grow* into more spiritual truths than Calvin had found and to correct his peculiar errors. It also caused a notable *lack of interest* in and *understanding* of the *prophetic* portions of the Bible, which has persisted to this day.

Calvin's Death and the Spread of His Doctrines

We will not attempt to cover in detail the spread of Calvinism, or the Reformed theology, to other lands, because the *doctrinal pattern* remained substantially the *same*. The same *spirit* guided the movement everywhere. Indeed, the Reformed churches to this day still bear the indelible stamp of Calvin's powerful mind and personality.

> From Geneva, Calvinism spread into France, Holland, England, Scotland, and New England. The pattern of Geneva could not be reproduced in these lands, at least not at the outset. A single city might be turned into a select community. In the case of an entire land this was a very difficult matter. Eventually the ideal was most nearly achieved in Scotland and New England (Bainton 121).

When we read of the *public whipping post* and of *burning people at the stake* in the "Puritan" New England settlements, we may realize that this was just a continuation of Calvin's system. As illustrated in New England, and with John Knox in Scotland, Calvin's adherents tried whenever possible to *rule* or at least *dominate* the political government and the entire population *by force*.

Even to the time of Calvin's death, his mind was alert and sharp, although his body was wasted with disease. When he felt his time had come, he sent for the Senate, in whose deliberations he had so often participated and dominated. He urged its members to *guard the state* from enemies who still threatened it.

Shortly after, he died peacefully. His fellow ministers were full of grief, for his great personality had inspired them all—and his death left a vacuum, which no one else could fill. His *dominant mind* and *personality* were such that "he excited the most profound *admiration* in some, and an equally profound *aversion* in others" (Fisher, *The History of the Christian Church* 329).

This very *dominance* of Luther and Calvin was, in many ways, detrimental. It led men to *accept without question* their doctrine and practice—never thinking to *prove* these ideas by the holy word of God.

Actually, as we have seen, many of the *tenets* and *actions* of the leading reformers are *as far removed* from the teaching and practice of Christ and the apostles as would seem possible in a civilized religious society!

Perhaps the Protestant doctrine was an improvement over the corruptions of the Roman church and its authoritarian popes. But *how much* of an improvement was it? Was it a genuine *restoration* of the *original* Christianity's *faith* and *practice*?

Even a respected Protestant historian has stated:

Protestantism deposed the infallible pope in a large part of Europe and it did well. It was, unfortunately, too much disposed to make *infallible popes of the Reformers* and to place *Luther* and *Calvin*, the infallible theologians, *in the place of Christ Himself* as an authority that could not be gainsaid. This tendency was, perhaps, its strength at a time of conflict, when it avails much to have intense beliefs and no doubts, to march and to battle at the word of command. It was a source of weakness and stagnation when the battle was over and theology became more a matter of accepted dogmas than a creed to live by and fight for. Calvinism, like Lutheranism, degenerated into a sort of scholasticism against which it had been, in part, a protest (MacKinnon 291).

As MacKinnon has wisely observed, Protestants today—instead of open-mindedly seeking for *more truth*—have "accepted dogmas," which they strive to defend in the manner of medieval scholastics. God commands us to "... *grow in the grace and knowledge of our Lord and Savior Jesus Christ*" (2 Peter 3:18).

Protestants often have tended to make *infallible popes* out of Luther, Calvin and the other early reformers. In the next chapter, we will continue this factual and gripping discussion with the shocking account of the real facts behind the Reformation in England and the tumultuous reign of Henry VIII.

Chapter 7

England Rebels Against Rome

The third key reformatory movement that needs to be considered as distinct in itself is the one that took place in England. It was a reformation by *force* even more so than that under John Calvin.

As we turn to consider the amazing *truth* about the Reformation in England, let us ask ourselves the same questions we did concerning the previous phases of this movement: Was this a return to the faith and practice of Jesus Christ and His Apostles? Was this, indeed, a return to "the BIBLE, the whole Bible, and nothing but the Bible"?

King Henry VIII and the English Revolt

The so-called "reformation" in England was due almost entirely to the actions of one man, Henry VIII. Since, under his influence, the English revolt produced no outstanding religious leaders and very few distinctive doctrines, a detailed analysis of its progress is not necessary for an understanding of its unique place in the Reformation as a whole. Yet, an understanding of its principal *origins* and *results* is important to aid our comprehension of its later influence on the English-speaking peoples of the world.

When Henry VIII ascended the throne of England in 1509, it was already an established royal policy for the kings to control most ecclesiastical appointments, and to fill many of the *chief political posts* with highly educated churchmen. Naturally, this led to many *abuses*, and often encouraged *greed*, *dishonesty* and *worldly shrewdness* in the higher clergy.

This situation also tended to subvert the religious allegiance normally felt by the Roman clergy toward Rome. It was replaced, through political office and interest, by a feeling of *national loyalty*. This was further strengthened by a growing national antagonism to all foreign encroachments, papal or otherwise (Walker, Williston 401).

Under such circumstances, it was not at all difficult for Henry VIII, a young, handsome, brilliant and vain monarch, to sway and intimidate the English Catholic clergy according to his whims.

Henry had inherited an ample treasury from his father, Henry VII, and enjoyed immense popularity with his subjects. But because of a political alliance with the Spanish, he had been pledged by his father to marry Catherine of Aragon, the daughter of Ferdinand and Isabella of Spain. Actually, she had first been his older brother's wife, though it was said that the marriage was never consummated before Arthur's early death.

Catherine was about six years older than Henry. Although this had seemed to make little difference at first, some fifteen years later the passionate, self-willed monarch found himself married to an overweight, prematurely aging woman of forty. It is known that, at this time, Henry satisfied his passions with a *series of mistresses* for many years, and this might have continued indefinitely but for two circumstances.

First, it appears that Henry became especially enamored of Anne Boleyn, and that she insisted on becoming his *wife*. Secondly, only one of the six children Catherine had borne him survived infancy—a girl, Mary. A woman *had never ruled England before*, and Henry may have feared that the absence of a male heir to the throne would lead to civil war. He wanted to wed another woman, and have a male heir (Hausser 170–171).

The Marriage Question

About the year 1526, Henry applied to Rome for a declaration annulling his marriage to Catherine. He based his appeal on the fact that she had first been his deceased brother's wife, and that a *papal dispensation* had been granted to allow him to marry her, as this relationship normally constituted an impediment to marriage according to Catholic law.

Henry *now* wished to have this dispensation, and consequently his marriage, declared invalid. He tried to gain the support of Thomas

Wolsey—whom he had made Lord Chancellor, and Pope Leo X had made a cardinal.

Up to this point, Wolsey had been Henry's right-hand man. But he was also the *pope's representative*, and was trying to protect himself by steering a middle course in the matter. Consequently, the matter was delayed—the pope and Wolsey hoping that Henry might change his mind.

This proceeding soon exhausted the king's patience, and he was advised by Thomas Cranmer and Thomas Cromwell to put his case before the universities of Europe. This Henry did, using *bribery* abroad and *threats* at home to gain a *partial* endorsement from some of the Protestant scholars and theologians for his divorce (Fisher, *The Reformation* 319).

In the meantime, Henry dismissed Cardinal Wolsey on *trumped-up charges*, and the disgraced cardinal fell ill and died on his way to be tried for *treason*. His death would not be the first in this matter. As events would demonstrate, Henry was willing to *kill* those who opposed his *unbridled lust* for women and power.

Henry now bullied the English Parliament into passing measures stating that he was "the Protector and *Supreme Head* of the Church and Clergy of England" after which was added, after a long debate, "as far as is permitted by the law of Christ." He then caused Parliament to pass laws forbidding the introduction of papal bulls into England, and cutting off the papal *revenues* from England (Fisher, *The Reformation* 320).

While his case was still pending at Rome, Henry rushed through a hasty divorce and secretly, though formally, married Anne Boleyn on January 25, 1533. It seems evident that he had *already entered into illegal, adulterous relations with her* because on September 7 of the same year she bore a daughter, Elizabeth, later to be queen (Walker, Williston 403).

Soon after, Henry's *new favorite*, Thomas Cranmer, was appointed as Archbishop of Canterbury. On May 23, he held an ecclesiastical court and formally adjudged Henry's marriage to Catherine *null* and *void*.

England's Break with Rome

The inevitable result of all these actions was soon forthcoming. On July 11, 1533, Pope Clement VII issued a bull excommunicating Henry. Henry replied in kind, and soon obtained from Parliament statutes *forbidding all payments* to the pope, directing that all bishops were now to be elected on the king's nomination, and doing away with all other recognition of papal authority (Fisher, *The Reformation* 320–321).

In November of 1534, Parliament passed the famous Supremacy Act. In it, Henry and his successors were declared "the only supreme head in earth of the Church of England," without any qualifying clauses, and with full power to redress "heresies" and "abuses" (Bettenson 322).

The break with Rome was now complete. Although it was primarily a matter of Henry's own *self-will*, it could not have been accomplished without the strong national feeling and dislike of papal authority already growing among the English people.

What made the breach with Rome irreparable was the policy Henry now proceeded upon, that of *confiscating the monasteries* and abbey lands, and *distributing* part of the *plundered wealth* among his courtiers and friends (Fisher, *The Reformation* 321).

> For his work, Henry had found a new agent in Thomas Cromwell (1485?–1540), a man of very humble origin, a soldier, merchant, and moneylender by turns, of whom Wolsey had made much use as a business and parliamentary agent. By 1531 Cromwell was of the privy council; in 1534 master of the rolls; and in 1536, layman that he was, vice-regent for the King in ecclesiastical affairs. Henry was hungry for ecclesiastical property, both to maintain his lavish court and to create and reward adherents—the Reformation everywhere was marked by these confiscations—and late in 1534 he commissioned Cromwell to have the monasteries visited and report on their condition. The alleged facts, the truth or falsity of which is still a disputed matter, were laid before Parliament, which in February, 1536, adjudged to the King, "his heirs and assigns forever, to do and use therewith his and their own wills," all monastic establishments having an income of less than two hundred pounds annually. The number thus sequestered was three hundred and seventy-six (Walker, Williston 404).

It is significant to note, as Walker states, that it was a common practice among the Protestant princes and nobles to *confiscate the wealth* of the Catholic Church whenever possible. It is evident that most of these influential "Protestants" were much more concerned with *enriching themselves* than with any theological changes that might be made. In fact, Henry's break with Rome resulted in practically *no change whatever* in doctrine, except the rejection of papal authority and the substitution of the English monarch as "head" of the church.

The entire situation developed primarily because of Henry's *sexual passion* and *lust for power—not* as a result of earnest men seeking to restore Scriptural truth.

Theological Developments

During this time, a number of religious leaders had been influenced by the work of the Reformation on the continent. One of them, William Tyndale, translated the New Testament into English. However, he was unable to have it published in England. Instead, it was published on the continent in 1526, and many copies found their way to England, although church and civil authorities tried to suppress it.

This placing of the Bible in the hands of the people helped prepare the way for later doctrinal changes along *Lutheran lines*. But for the time being, the Roman Catholic dogma was to be enforced (Walker, Williston 404–405).

King Henry's own religious attitude, except towards the papacy, was that of *Catholic orthodoxy*. At times, he would make limited doctrinal concessions to please the German Protestants when he needed their support. But in 1539, because of fears of France and Spain, Henry induced Parliament to pass the Six Articles Act. It maintained a strict doctrine of transubstantiation, vows of chastity, auricular confession, and other *Catholic* practices (Fisher, *The Reformation* 324).

Meanwhile, however, he proceeded to complete the *confiscation* of all the monasteries in 1539, and strengthen his position as head of the church and state. His *sharing* of the *seized wealth* of the ecclesiastical properties built up the fortunes of the Protestant ruling class, whose *personal interests* now lay in continued separation from Rome.

The true fact is that they were *Catholics in doctrine*, but Protestant in their confirmation of Henry's right to substitute himself for the pope as head of the church and to share with them the *booty of the plundered monasteries*.

King Henry's Marital Escapades

As "supreme head" of the Church of England, Henry's conduct toward his enemies and, strangely, even toward his wives, was *as far removed* from Christian principles as would seem possible.

In the summer of 1535, he cruelly *executed* two of England's ablest scholars and theologians, Bishop John Fisher and Sir Thomas More, because they refused to endorse his supremacy over the church and clergy of England. Many other notable persons paid *with their lives* for disagreeing with Henry's views.

A helpful summary of Henry's vicious conduct toward his wives, and nobles, is given by Alzog:

> Henry was as atrociously cruel to his wives as he was to his ministers and other subjects of inferior degree. Catharine of Aragon survived her repudiation a little less than three years, dying a most exemplary death, January 8, 1536. She was hardly laid in her grave, when Anne Boleyn, who had taken her place in her husband's affections, and was the cause of all her misfortunes, was tried on the charges of adultery, incest and high treason, declared guilty, and beheaded on the green within the Tower, May 19, 1536. Cranmer, who had formerly "in virtue of his apostolic authority" pronounced the marriage between Henry and Anne lawful and valid, was now called upon to reverse his former decision, and, *"in the name of Christ and for the glory of God,"* declared that the same marriage was and always had been null and void. On the day of Anne's execution, as if to express his contempt for her memory, Henry dressed himself in a suit of white, and on the following morning was married to Jane Seymour, who died (October 24, 1537) in less than a fortnight after giving birth to a male child, subsequently known as Edward VI. Henry was next married to Anne of Cleves in the beginning of the year 1540. The marriage was a political one, brought about through the agency of Thomas Cromwell, who hoped to strengthen the Protestant cause in England, and prop up his own power through the influence of the new queen, who was known to be a thorough-going Lutheran. Deceived as to her beauty and personal attractions, Henry married her only

because he could not well help himself, and, after living with her six months, procured a divorce mainly on these grounds (July 13). Within a month (August 8) he married Catherine Howard, who, being shortly after charged with having committed adultery, was pronounced guilty, and beheaded February 13, 1541. Henry's sixth and last wife, Catharine Parr, was on one occasion nearly losing her head for venturing to differ on theological questions with the Head of the Church of England; but quickly detecting her mistake, she escaped the royal vengeance by adroitly flattering his great wisdom and theological learning, expressing her most humble submission to his judgment, and professing that in differing from him she had only desired to draw him into a heated discussion, because when animated, he seemed to forget the pain of the malady from which he was suffering. By this clever expedient, Catharine kept her head on her shoulders, and had the good fortune to outlive the brutal monster, who died in 1547.

Henry reigned for thirty-eight years, and during that time he ordered the execution of two queens, two cardinals, two archbishops, eighteen bishops, thirteen abbots, five hundred priors and monks, thirty-eight doctors of divinity and laws, twelve dukes and earls, one hundred and sixty-four gentlemen, one hundred and twenty-four commoners, and one hundred and ten ladies (Alzog 322–323).

Protestantism Advanced Under Edward VI

At the death of Henry VIII, the great body of Englishmen stood with the late king in desiring *no considerable change* in doctrine or worship (Walker, Williston 408). But *despite* this fact, England was to witness the introduction of many *Lutheran* teachings during the reign of Edward VI.

Upon his ascension, Edward was *only nine years of age*. The Duke of Somerset was immediately created *Protector* and headed the governmental council. He was a man of *Protestant sympathies* and was a friend of the dispossessed lower agricultural classes.

Under the influence of Somerset and Archbishop Cranmer, a number of changes in doctrine and worship were introduced.

It was at this time that the Six Articles were repealed and the real *basic doctrines* of the Church of England were framed. Cranmer was a thorough-going Protestant in his sympathies, and brought over a number of *Lutheran theologians* for advice and counsel.

Laws enforcing the celibacy of the priesthood were now repealed. Communion with both the bread and wine for the congregation was introduced, following Luther. The use of English in the church services was made mandatory, and help in formulating prayer books and liturgies was given by the continental reformers (Fisher, *The History of the Christian Church* 357–358).

During this period, the basis of English Protestantism was definitely established. But, as we have seen, it was the Protestantism of the *German reformers* that was brought in on a limited scale.

Bloody Queen Mary's Reign

The plans for reformation came to an abrupt halt with the early death of Edward VI in 1553, and the accession of the Catholic Queen Mary. Because of the conniving of some of the Protestant noblemen, Mary even had the sympathies of most of her subjects when she came to the throne (Walker, Williston 405).

Mary proceeded with caution at first upon the astute advice of her cousin, Emperor Charles V. Before long, *Parliament reversed itself* and declared the marriage of her mother to Henry valid. The whimsical attitude of the monarchs and political leaders of England toward the marriage state is appalling. Their actions are but a *shameful parody* of Christ's words: "Therefore what God has joined together, let not man separate" (Mark 10:9).

Also, these actions certainly indicate that the *hearts* of the British people were *not strongly persuaded* about their new Protestant "faith" at all. As one English scholar cynically comments, "With Parliament, Mary had no difficulty. As a contemporary ironically observed, they would have voted the establishment of the *Mahometan religion* with equal alacrity and zeal at the bidding of the Queen" (Babington, 286).

With *little opposition*, Mary persuaded Parliament to repeal the ecclesiastical legislation passed under Edward's reign, and public worship was restored to the forms of the last year of Henry VIII. But Cranmer was now *imprisoned*, and many of the more earnest Protestants fled to the continent.

At this time also, Mary contracted a marriage with the son of Emperor Charles V, Philip—who would soon become Philip II of Spain. Fear of Catholic and Spanish domination made this an exceedingly *unpopular marriage* with Mary's subjects, and she lost much public support through this action (Fisher, *The History of the Christian Church* 359).

The English nobles now feared the loss of the church property they had *seized*, and a series of mutinous uprisings took place. During much of this time, it was difficult to tell whether their Protestant sympathies or their English *nationalism* provoked these incidents (Hausser 569).

"Bloody" Mary now began the extermination of her enemies, and in February, 1554, *fifty people were hanged*. The entirely innocent Lady Jane Grey and her husband, Lord Guildford Dudley, were both *executed* for alleged conspiracy against the crown. Mary had never regarded her sister Elizabeth with much affection, so she was imprisoned in the Tower of London. But through all these years, Elizabeth prudently avoided anything that would arouse Mary's suspicion of her, and so kept her life (Hausser 570–573).

Even at the beginning of this persecution, the English nobles and Parliament were still ready to *give up their Protestantism* and "to regulate the Church and her doctrine in accordance with the Pope's pleasure if no one would interfere with the *distribution of Church property*..." (Hausser 571). It should certainly be plain that these nobles were more concerned with their *lust* for wealth and power than they were in trying to find true religion.

Once Mary allowed the erstwhile Protestants to keep the *seized church property*, Parliament readily consented to render obedience to the pope and to renew the edicts against heretics. Now those who continued to oppose the Roman religion began to be persecuted in full force. In the three years before Mary's death, about 270 Protestant "heretics" were *burned at the stake*, among whom were 55 women and four children (Hausser 571).

Many of these common people were faithful to their Protestant convictions to the end. Their spiritual leader, Thomas Cranmer, who had been Archbishop of Canterbury under Henry VIII and Edward VI, was not quite as constant. He *recanted* his Protestant sympathies under Queen Mary, in hope of *saving his life*. But once it was determined that he should die anyway, his courage revived. He disavowed his former recantation, declared that he was a Protestant, and died with dignity. "What course he would have pursued had he been permitted to live, it is *impossible* to tell..." (Babington 328).

Under Mary, the government prosecuted the Protestants like criminals. This naturally developed a *hatred of Rome* among the English people. *Not* because of true religious feeling, but in a *political sense*, the idea now arose that "Protestantism and English nationality were *identical*" (Hausser 573).

Thus, when we read of the staunch "Protestant" sentiment among the English peoples, we need to realize *why*. It became a spirit of English nationalism in opposition to Rome and a *national religion* that has persisted in England to our day. And, as many have perceived, its course has always depended more on *politics* and *power* than on sincere religious motives.

The English people continued in a partial state of *rebellion* until their Catholic Queen Mary died in November 1558. The nation now welcomed her sister, Elizabeth, to the throne (Fisher, *The History of the Christian Church* 362).

English Protestantism Established

Elizabeth soon established herself, as Henry VIII had done, as head of the Church of England. But, since the title "Supreme Head" had seemed objectionable to Catholics, she was now styled "Supreme Governor" of the national church (Walker, Williston 414).

Now, step by step, the Protestant principles formerly established under Edward VI were reintroduced. By the Act of Uniformity, 1559, the Prayer Book of Edward VI was restored for use in all the churches. All persons were *required* to attend the national church under penalty and fine, except for "lawful or reasonable excuse" (Moncrief 339).

Babington comments upon the *hypocritical changeableness* of the "religious" situation in England during this time.

> Thus within the space of a few years the English Parliament for the *third time* formally *recanted* its religious belief. It is vain to give any creditable reason for this amazing fact. To suppose that in making these changes the hereditary legislators and the representatives of the English people were swayed by spiritual zeal or religious conviction would be the *height of absurdity* (Babington 299).

Although Queen Elizabeth herself *dominated* in religious as well as civil affairs, Matthew Parker was now consecrated as Archbishop of Canterbury. Under his direction, the 42 *articles of faith* originally formulated by Thomas Cranmer were reduced to 39. In 1571, Parliament adopted them as the *basis of doctrine* of the Church of England. They set forth "a type of doctrine midway between Lutheranism and Calvinism" (Kurtz 315).

Actually, the religious *basis* of the Church of England was more of a *mixture* of Lutheranism, Calvinism and Catholicism. But the Thirty-Nine Articles were primarily based on *Lutheran* confessions of faith (Moncrief, p. 339). And, of course, *Luther's* theory of justification by faith *alone* was held. Yet *Calvin's* doctrines on the "Lord's Supper" and on *predestination* were, in the main, accepted.

But *many* Roman Catholic *rituals*, *customs* and *concepts* were retained. "The Thirty-Nine Articles contain many Protestant dogmas, but they also retain *much of the Roman cult*" (Moncrief 340).

Although there have been *some alterations* from time to time, the *doctrines* and *form of religion* established at this time under Queen Elizabeth remain *essentially the same* to this day in the Church of England (Wharey 240).

Summary

It is not our purpose in the present work to go into a detailed history of the various splits and divisions of the *three* main Protestant "trees." As we have already seen, *Luther's doctrines* spread over most of northern Germany, from there primarily to the Scandinavian countries, and then to the New World. *Calvin's theology* eventually dominated in Switzerland, parts of France and Germany, the Netherlands and Scotland. Later, it also found its way—with adaptations—to America, particularly the New England states.

As a *guiding principle*, it is important to realize that *every major Protestant body* must rightfully recognize as its legitimate ancestor one of these *key* reform movements. And Lutheranism, Calvinism, and Anglicanism must acknowledge that they *all* came, in the first place, from the Church of Rome.

Referring again to England, we may safely state that the three main churches rising out of the "puritan" movement of the seventeenth century—the Presbyterian, the Congregational, and the

Baptist—all owe to *Calvin* the major part of their *doctrines, customs* and *concepts*.

The later Methodist movement under John and Charles Wesley did *not* involve any change in the *basic doctrines* of the Church of England. It was only intended as a reformation *within* the Anglican Church, rejecting predestination and emphasizing personal holiness and a consciousness of a "witness of the Spirit" in the believer (Hurlbut 177).

To the end of his life, Wesley urged his followers to *remain in* the Church of England, declaring, "I live and die a *member* of the Church of England; and none who regard my judgment will ever separate from it" (Bettenson 361).

So, it is clear that even the Church of England, sprung from Rome, herself is a parent of other religious bodies holding *the same basic doctrines*. The point we wish to emphasize is that *all* of the major splits and divisions within Protestant "Christendom" *agreed* upon most of their *basic doctrines, traditions* and religious *concepts*. The significance of this will be considered later.

As we have seen, the English revolt was conceived in the *lust* and *sin* of Henry VIII. It was promoted among the people by a spirit of *nationalism* and *antagonism* toward Rome. It was helped to success by the *greed* of the English nobility for the wealth of the Catholic monasteries and lands. And it was placed on the throne by the royal realization of the *unchecked power* it conferred upon the English monarchs.

One eminent Protestant historian, Williston Walker, admits: "The remarkable feature of the *English revolt* is that it produced no outstanding religious leader—no Luther, Zwingli, Calvin or Knox. Nor did it, before the beginning of Elizabeth's reign, manifest any considerable spiritual awakening among the people. Its impulses were *political* and *social*" (Walker, Williston 415).

Let us face *honestly* and *squarely* the questions: Was this a return to pure New Testament Christianity? Was it a Spirit-led restoration of the "faith once delivered"? In the following chapter, the real *meaning* of all that we have discussed, and the *answers* to these questions, will be made plain. We need to *know* where today's Protestant "Christianity" really came from—and where it is headed!

Chapter 8

The Shocking Violence of the Reformers

S tartling though it seems, most of us have never really *proved* why we believe the things we do—especially those things about God and eternity!

Why is this so?

It is because of a quirk of human nature that makes us tend to *assume* that whatever our parents, friends, and associates tell us is completely *true*. And, once we have carelessly accepted from them various ideas and beliefs, we hate to *change* or to consider that *we may be wrong!*

Thus, the plain facts of history we have reviewed seem shocking to many who have previously *assumed* that what is called "Christianity" today is in truth the religion taught by Jesus Christ and His Apostles. But this is decidedly *not* the case! We can now say that the biblical and historical *proof* of this statement has been *abundantly demonstrated*. It is something every sincere person must *face squarely*!

Let us not blind our eyes to the meaning of truth!

Having reviewed the *facts* from authentic history, let us now probe the motives and methods of the Protestant reformers in the light of the book they profess to believe, the Holy Bible.

The Bible and the Reformation

We have examined the basic *foundations* of the Protestant churches today. We have gone to the *source* of the "divided Christendom" of our time.

If there is any one thing that all religionists agree upon, it is in lamenting the fact that the Protestant reformers have bequeathed to us a religious "Babylon" of monstrous proportions. For, as we have seen, nearly every major Protestant denomination must trace its history—directly or indirectly—from the Reformation of the sixteenth century. Until that time, their *religious ancestors* were all within the pale of the Roman Catholic Church.

Jesus Christ said, "I will build *My church...*" (Matthew 16:18). We can only imagine His reaction at seeing hundreds of *differing* churches all laying claim to His name and approbation.

We wonder what might be the judgment of Christ's faithful apostle Paul, who urged us "to keep the *unity* of the Spirit in the bond of peace," and was inspired to state, "There is *one body* and one Spirit, just as you were called in one hope of your calling; one Lord, one faith, one baptism; one God and Father of all, who is above all, and through all, and in you all" (Ephesians 4:3–6).

Needless to say, this unity is *not to be found* in the Protestant world today. There are *many* faiths, and *many* bodies, or churches. All too often, they express the *antagonism* that Luther felt toward the Swiss reformers: "Yours is a *different spirit*... We cannot acknowledge you as brethren" (Schaff 7: 645).

Jesus said, "You will know them by their *fruits*" (Matthew 7:16). It is an *undeniable fact* that the "fruit" of the Protestant Reformation is the *divided "churchianity"* of our day. We must say at the outset that this is *bad fruit*.

Paul tells us that the Spirit of God produces *unity*—not division. Therefore, we should examine in retrospect to see what the spirit was, and what the *motivating factors* were, that produced the religious *confusion* resulting from the Reformation.

Nationalism and Lust

We have seen how the spirit of *nationalism* was growing throughout Europe just prior to the Reform movement. The people of Europe were tired of the religious and financial oppressions of Rome.

Therefore, Luther immediately gained a large following among the German nobles and middle class when he cried, "We were born to be *masters*.... It is time the *glorious, Teutonic people* should cease to be the puppet of the Roman pontiff" (Bettenson 278). And we have seen how the English nobility were wedded to Henry VIII's "reformation" *because* they had been allowed to *seize the wealth* of the monastic lands and establishments. But in the latter case, as we have noted, their Parliamentary representatives *changed* their "religion" *three times* and "would have voted the establishment of the Mohametan religion" at the monarch's bidding.

And it was the *sexual lust* of Henry VIII for Anne Boleyn that very clearly marks the starting point of the English revolt against Rome.

Of course, there is *no doubt* that many thousands of the common people in all of these countries sincerely desired not only a release from the tyranny of Rome, but also a restoration of religious truth and religious freedom. But *people follow their leaders.*

So, the real question is not what *might* have happened, but what *did* happen, and what motivated the political and religious *leaders* of the Reformation.

"In the end, it was a *national system* of Reformation that was carried out.... In those countries in which the *national* and *political* stimulus was absent or was weak, the religious movement failed" (Plummer 16).

So, we see that the spirit of nationalism was a *major factor* in helping the Reformation to succeed. It is important to realize that this very *exaltation of nations* has now resulted in the threat of *human annihilation* in our time!

For *political, financial,* and *nationalistic* reasons, men revolted against the Church of Rome. They exalted private judgment and reason. And in place of the Roman authority, which had been thought to represent *God,* they placed *nationalistic authority*—and the *gods of war!*

It is true that Luther and Calvin had personal religious motivations. As we have described, Luther's mind was tortured with a perpetual sense of *guilt.* In his extreme emphasis on salvation by faith *alone,* he was trying desperately to devise some system where the *law* of God and the *justice* of God would have no place.

But Luther's *personal* spiritual upheaval would have had little effect on Germany or the world had he not appealed to the *political* and *financial* instincts of the German princes. And "it is true to say that the motives which led to the Lutheran revolt were to a large extent *secular* rather than spiritual" (Plummer 9).

And while the reforms under Luther and Calvin contained an element of religious conviction in the spiritual leaders, they primarily employed the *materialistic grievances* of the princes and the people as a stimulus to rebel against Rome. It was a spirit of *nationalism,* which assured the widespread success of these movements.

Violent Methods of the Reformers

When it came to a showdown, the Protestant reformers were as ready to resort to *violence, bloodshed,* and *persecution* as their Roman Catholic adversaries. In any discussion of the *methods* by which the Reformation triumphed, this fact must be acknowledged.

We have already seen how Luther *won* the German princes to his cause. How he *used* them to fight Catholicism and to *persecute* those who disagreed with him, is another matter. The same principle may apply to Zwingli and Calvin and the political councils under their sway, and to King Henry VIII and his subservient Parliament and nobility.

Do we remember Luther's raving appeal to the German princes to *"smite, strangle,* and *stab,* secretly or publicly"* those peasants who had applied the principle of his teachings to their own circumstances? Do we remember that he reversed himself in 1529, and said that Christians were "bound" to *resort to arms* to defend their Protestant beliefs?

It is also a fact that Luther *approved* the *persecution* and *martyrdom* of the Anabaptists and other sects who rejected his teachings. Commenting on the *beheading* of Anabaptists in Saxony, he said that "their courage showed that they were possessed by the devil" (Plummer 174).

The same treatment was given those who did not go along with the *national church system,* which was *forced* upon the English people. Besides the *several hundred* nobles and commoners who lost their lives through the personal and religious bigotry of Henry VIII, many hundreds of others lost their lives under the reign of his Protestant daughter, Elizabeth I.

Those who refused to acknowledge the *religious supremacy* of the English monarch were dealt with as if they were guilty of high treason. "Before 1588, *twelve hundred* Catholics had already fallen victims to the persecution. In England alone, during the last twenty years of Elizabeth's reign, one hundred and forty-two priests were hanged, drawn, and quartered, for their faith. Ninety priests and religious [persons] died in prison, one hundred and five were banished for life, and sixty-two laymen of consideration suffered martyrdom" (Deharbe 484).

And it was not just the monarchs who practiced intolerance in England, but the *Protestant religious leaders* as well. During the reign of young King Edward VI, Archbishop Cranmer persuaded him to sign the *death warrant* of two Anabaptists, one of them a *woman*. They were *burned at the stake*. In relating this, Schaff tells us: "The English Reformers were not behind those of the Continent in the matter of *intolerance*" (Schaff 711).

After Calvinism was introduced into Scotland, those who professed the Catholic religion were subject to the *death penalty*, and many paid with their lives for their religious beliefs (Deharbe 485).

Remember that these people were victims of *Protestant* persecution!

By appealing to *financial* or *nationalistic* motives, and by getting into and *dominating* the *political power*, the leading Protestant reformers were able to *force* their doctrines on the common people. Before gaining *political power*, the reformers all insisted upon the *inalienable right* of every Christian to search the Bible for himself, and to judge its teachings independently (Deharbe 620). But once they were in power, *woe* be to the Catholic, the Anabaptist, or to any other who continued to insist upon this inalienable right!

As we have seen, it was the *same picture* under John Calvin's "theocracy" in Geneva, Switzerland. Fisher states: "Not only profaneness and drunkenness, but innocent amusements and the teaching of divergent theological doctrines, were *severely punished*" (Fisher, *The History of the Church* 325). We have already catalogued some of the many *hundreds* of instances where people were subjected to *imprisonment*, to *public whipping,* or to the death penalty because of some innocent amusement, or because they *disagreed* with John Calvin's religious ideas.

But *one instance* stands out, which was defended by almost *all* the reformers of that day. It is one that we should especially remember as an outstanding example of the *reasoning* of the early reformers on the subject of religious *toleration*. It is the martyrdom of Michael Servetus.

The Burning of Michael Servetus

Servetus was a man about the same age as Calvin. Although he was born in Spain, he practiced medicine in France and is said to have anticipated Harvey's discovery of the circulation of blood. When still a young man, he published a book on the "errors of the Trinity." In it, he disagreed with the common doctrine of God as a Trinity, held by Catholics *and* Protestants alike. His position was similar to that held by those of the Unitarian belief today (Plummer 170).

For teaching and writing about this doctrine, and also for holding a divergent view on the exact nature of Christ's divinity, he was hated and persecuted by Catholics and Protestants alike.

Fleeing from the Catholic Inquisition at Vienna, France, he foolishly passed through Protestant Geneva. Someone recognized him and reported his presence to Calvin, who had him arrested and imprisoned (Plummer 172).

As Servetus' trial began before the Calvin-dominated Council, John Calvin wrote to a fellow reformer, "I hope that the judgment will be sentence of *death*..." (Plummer 172).

Plummer continues:

At the trial Calvin acted as prosecutor and had no trouble in causing Servetus to incriminate himself hopelessly.... It is one of the many painful features in the case that it was distinctly to Calvin's interest to get Servetus condemned, for such a triumph would greatly strengthen his position in Geneva. The case dragged on, and, as in the case of Bolsec, there was much correspondence with other authorities, both ecclesiastical and civil, in Switzerland. In the end it seemed to be clear that Calvin's enemies had failed, and that Protestant feeling was in favor of removing such a pest as Servetus from the earth. On October 26, he was sentenced, to be burned alive the next day. Calvin asked for a milder form of death, but his request was refused. Through the clumsiness of the executioner, the agonies of Servetus were prolonged. His last cry was "Jesus, Thou Son of the Eternal God, have pity on me," and it has been noticed that "eternal" is the epithet, not of the Son, but of God. The book for which Servetus was condemned was tied to his neck to be burned with him. It fell off, and was rescued from the flames. It may still be seen, a ghastly memorial of Reformation "ethics," in the National Library at Paris.

We have always to remember that in putting Servetus to death, neither Calvin nor the Council nor the Swiss Governments whom they consulted, had any jurisdiction whatever. Their action was lynch law of the most revolting kind (Plummer 172–173).

We notice that even the Protestant historian is forced to acknowledge that one of the *two greatest* of the Protestant reformers resorted to an illegal "lynch law" procedure in order to *destroy* a religious antagonist!

The blunt *truth* is that this was nothing but "*respectable*" *murder!*

Jesus Christ said to "*love* your enemies, *bless* those who curse you, do *good* to those who hate you, and *pray* for those who spitefully use you and persecute you" (Matthew 5:44).

The Apostle Paul was inspired to write, "Beloved, *do not avenge yourselves*, but rather give place to wrath; for it is written, 'Vengeance *is* Mine, I will repay,' says the Lord. Therefore 'If your *enemy* is hungry, *feed him*'" (Romans 12:19–20).

In very clearly indicating that the right of civil judging or condemning to death of others in spiritual matters was *not given* to fallible human beings, Jesus *freed* the woman taken in adultery (John 8:11). He commanded, "*Judge not*, that you be not judged" (Matthew 7:1).

Did John Calvin know these scriptures? Did he understand these principles, which nearly all civilized men have since come to acknowledge?

How Could Calvin Make Such a Choice?

The Protestant historians answer: "He easily takes the *lead* among the systematic expounders of the Reformed system of Christian doctrine.... Calvin's theology is based upon a thorough knowledge of the Scriptures" (Schaff 8: 260–261).

Here was a man who really *knew* the Bible. He wrote learned commentaries upon it and was thoroughly familiar with the teaching and example of Christ and the inspired New Testament Church.

Yet he was willing not only to condemn, but to *directly cause* a man to be *burned to death* for disagreeing with his religious doctrines. In the absolute sense of everything that Jesus Christ taught, stood for, and lived for, John Calvin stands condemned as a *murderer!* But did he *mean* to be? Was he *sincere*? Or was it a *rash act* carried out in the heat of passion?

To the last question we may answer in the *negative*. For after plenty of time for mature consideration, John Calvin sought to *defend* this vile act and *justify* himself. And, remarkable as it may seem, so did *many* of the other leading reformers!

In the year after the burning of Servetus, Calvin dogmatically asserted, "Whoever shall now contend that it is unjust to put heretics and blasphemers *to death* will knowingly and willingly incur their very guilt. This is not laid down on human authority; it is God who speaks and prescribes a *perpetual rule* for his Church" (Schaff 8: 791).

It is a *sobering truth* that if John Calvin's kind of "perpetual rule" against heretics were carried out today, *very few* of us would long remain alive!

Fortunately for his name, Luther was not living to pronounce a judgment in favor of Servetus' burning. Knowing his past record, however, it is almost *certain* that he would have agreed with Calvin in putting Servetus to death.

However, Luther's closest associate and advisor, Philip Melanchthon, was quick to express his *agreement* with Calvin. He later wrote Bullinger, another of the Swiss reformers: "I judge also that the Genevese senate did *perfectly right*, to put an end to this obstinate man, who could never cease blaspheming. And I wonder at those who disapprove of this severity" (Schaff 8: 707).

Thus, we see that the German reformers *agreed* with the Swiss in *burning to death* a man *simply because he disagreed with their theological opinions!*

We have asked if Calvin could be *sincere* in all of this. It is a difficult question, the *complete* answer to which *only* God knows. The human mind sometimes plays tricks on us. We often *willfully overlook* those things we don't wish to acknowledge. As we shall soon see, it is evident that both Luther and Calvin did this in the development of their doctrines and in some of their actions as well.

However, judging from the facts at our disposal, and from contemporary testimony, it appears that Calvin *meant* to be sincere. Within his own sphere of thinking, Calvin was somehow sincere in feeling that it was right to *burn Servetus* for religious disagreement, even though he and the other reformers claimed the freedom of the individual conscience in their struggle with Rome.

The Reason for Protestant Violence and Persecutions

The answer to the killing of Servetus, then, does not lie in rashness later repented of, nor does it lie in a complete lack of sincerity on Calvin's part. But what *is* the answer?

The same answer is given, in essence, by many Protestant historians. It is one that *every* honest student of the Bible and history must acknowledge.

The *answer* is that, even long after their separation from Rome and their "conversion" to Protestantism, the early reformers and their followers were still literally *saturated* with the *doctrines*, the *concepts*, and the *practices* of their "*mother*" *church* at Rome. "The reformers *inherited* the doctrine of *persecution* from their mother church, and practiced it as far as they had the power. They fought intolerance with intolerance. They differed favorably from their opponents in the degree and extent, but *not* in the *principle*, of intolerance" (Schaff 8: 700).

As we shall see, this frank admission by Schaff reveals why so *many* of the Protestant doctrines and actions seem so totally inconsistent with their avowed intention of basing everything on "nothing but the Bible."

We have seen that Martin Luther *played politics*, *condoned bigamy*, counseled a *lie*, and encouraged the *slaughter* of peasants and *execution* of Anabaptists (which included *drowning* many of them).

It has been shown that the English revolt began with the *lust* of Henry VIII, and that he and Queen Elizabeth *and* their Protestant theologians all had a part in *slaughtering* hundreds of Catholic, Anabaptist and, later, Puritan dissenters.

Now we have reviewed the part that John Calvin and the Swiss reformers played in the *persecution* of Anabaptists and in the cruel *punishment* and *execution* of their own Genevese citizens for failing to conform in all respects to Calvin's doctrine. Finally, we have described the *agreement* of nearly *all* the early Protestant leaders in the "lynch law" of execution by *burning at the stake,* which Calvin inflicted upon Michael Servetus for *purely religious reasons.*

We have *proved* that these were "cold-blooded" killings. They were *not* the result of the passion of the moment, nor were those responsible afflicted by *temporary insanity.*

These *crimes* in the name of religion were *calculated* beforehand, and they were still *defended* by theological argument long after they had occurred!

We have seen that the *real explanation* lies in the fact that the early reformers "inherited" *much* of the *doctrine* and *spirit* of their "mother" church. They were as men *spiritually drunk*—unable to see clearly the real *meaning* and *outcome* of their teachings and actions!

In the following chapter, we propose to reveal the actual *purpose* behind the Protestant movement—and the startling *reason* behind the religious *confusion* and spiritual *drunkenness* bequeathed to our generation.

The facts contained in this book have a direct bearing on *your* life and *your* future! Ask God for an *open* mind.

Chapter 9

The True Meaning of the Reformation

There is a basic but little understood reason for the pitiful state of religious *confusion* that now exists! It is time *you* really understood that reason. It is time you honestly faced the **truth!**

We sometimes hear modern religious leaders lament the fact that there exists such a veritable Babylon of modern religious denominations and sects—all calling themselves "Christian." They may even admit that Jesus Christ founded only *one* Church—not hundreds of differing religious groups politically organized and directed by men.

Much of this Babylon of conflicting religious denominations was spawned by the Protestant reformers. We need to understand the *reason* for this pathetic outcome of their efforts.

Instead of *assuming* the beliefs we have been taught are true, as so many people do, we need to *"prove* **all** things" in the light of God's word, the Holy Bible. We need to honestly face the question of whether the Protestant Reformation was *in any way* inspired of God. And we must *have* **proof** for our beliefs!

As you read this final chapter, may the living God help *you* to *open your mind* to the possibility that *you may have been deceived* in the past!

With the constant threat of World War III and world suicide, we are nearing the prophesied *end* of this age (Matthew 24:21–22). *Knowledge* is now being increased (Daniel 12:4).

Will *you* sincerely "prove *all* things," and quit assuming? Will you walk in the light as God gives it? Will you **obey** the truth as God opens your mind to understand it?

Let us again ask ourselves: Was this a return to the biblical faith and practice of Jesus Christ and His Apostles?

Protestant Contradictions

While this publication is not designed or intended to include arguments about the hundreds of differing Protestant doctrines and creeds, we do wish to consider the *principles* which guided the reformers in coming to their conclusions. Indeed, we have already outlined the basic doctrines upon which the Reformation was based. But now we wish to examine more thoroughly their origins and results, and to examine the essential *nature* of Protestantism as a whole.

We remember Chillingworth's claim: "The *Bible*, the whole Bible, and *nothing but the Bible*, is the religion of Protestants." We recall the Protestant affirmation of the Scriptures as "the inspired rule of faith and practice."

Fisher tells us, "Protestantism, under whatever diversities of form it appeared, and notwithstanding the varieties of character and of opinion which are observed among its leaders, is distinguished as a system of belief by two principles. These are justification by faith alone, and the exclusive authority of the Scriptures" (Fisher, *The Reformation* 459).

Most Protestants have grown up *believing* these statements are *true*. What most people do *not* realize is that Luther, Calvin, and the English reformers rejected entire books of the Bible or else completely dismissed their real authority. And they forced their interpretations onto countless scriptures where the natural meaning did not conform to their preconceived doctrines.

We recall that Martin Luther was so oppressed with a persistent feeling of guilt that he wanted to overthrow every verse in the Bible which taught that *obedience* is required for salvation *in addition to faith*. He insisted that we are saved by faith *alone*. So convicted was Luther of this idea that he purposefully introduced the word "alone" into his translation of Romans 3:28, so that it says we are justified by "faith *alone*"—something the original Greek *does not say!* The only defense he provided for this defiant act of adding to God's word was his presumptuous statement, "It is the will of Dr. Martin Luther that it should be so" (Alzog 3: 199).

Especially in regard to his insistence on faith *alone* and his *rejection* of countless scriptures teaching the need for *obedience*, Luther was a stubborn, self-willed man.

The Bible teaches: "Sin is the transgression of the law" (1 John 3:4, *KJV*). This is clearly speaking of the spiritual law written by the very finger of God—the *Ten Commandments*. The inspired James explains this: "For whoever shall keep the whole law, and yet stumble in one point, he is guilty of all. For He who said, 'Do not commit adultery,' also said, 'Do not murder.' Now if you do not commit adultery, but you do murder, you have become a transgressor of the law. So speak and so do as those who will be judged by the law of liberty" (James 2:10–12).

What law forbids adultery and killing? Obviously, it is the Ten Commandments to which James refers. And he concludes by telling us to *speak* and *act* according to this law.

This agrees with the words of Jesus Christ, for when a young man came to ask Him the way to eternal life, He answered: "But if you want to enter into life, keep the commandments," and He proceeded to name some of the Ten Commandments (Matthew 19:16–19).

Completely ignoring the direct parallel between the teaching of James and of Jesus Christ, Luther haughtily declared: "Compared with the Epistles of St. Paul, this is in truth *an epistle of straw*; it contains absolutely *nothing* to remind one of the style of the Gospel" (Alzog 3: 208). Thus, Luther stubbornly *rejected* the entire book of James because it did not agree with his doctrines!

In rejecting the first five books of the Bible, Luther declared: "We have no wish either to see or hear Moses. Let us *leave Moses to the Jews*, to whom he was given to serve as a Mirror of Saxony; he has nothing in common with Pagans and Christians, and *we should take no notice of him*" (Alzog 3: 207).

Since Luther regarded Moses as having to do with God's law—which Luther hated—he wished to have nothing to do with Moses' inspired writings!

But since Paul was Luther's favorite writer, we wonder what his reaction was to Paul's inspired reminder to Timothy that "from childhood you have known the Holy Scriptures, which are able to make you wise for salvation through faith which is in Christ Jesus. All Scripture is given by inspiration of God..." (2 Timothy 3:15–16). Remember that only the *Old* Testament Scriptures were written when Timothy was a child.

And, since Luther stubbornly wished to "take no notice" of Moses, we might remind him of the Apostle John's description of the victorious saints of God singing "the song of *Moses*, the servant of God, and the song of the Lamb" (Revelation 15:3). But Luther's own writings promptly answer: "I look upon the revelations of John to be neither Apostolic nor prophetic" (Michelet 273). He might then add: "Everyone may form his own judgment of this book; as for myself, I feel an *aversion* to it, and *to me this is sufficient reason for rejecting it*" (Alzog 3: 208).

It is a *fact* that Martin Luther willfully *rejected* the authority of any book in the Bible to which he felt an "aversion."

Now, perhaps, we begin to understand the real meaning of the religious confusion of our time. Modern Protestants have inherited from Martin Luther—acknowledged as the *greatest leader* of the Reformation—a spirit of *self-will* and a willingness to *reject* the supreme *authority* of God's word!

Seeing the foolishness and futility of the Roman Catholic penitential system, Martin Luther had rebelled against the idea of any "works." But he had grown up as a Roman Catholic, was trained and schooled as a Catholic priest, and was *filled* with the Catholic concept of law and works.

Being, therefore, in a condition that amounted to *spiritual drunkenness*, he was *unable* to see clearly the difference between the *Bible* teaching of *obedience* to spiritual commandments, and the *Jewish* and *Roman Catholic* teaching of subservience to physical "works" and to man-made ecclesiastical laws and traditions.

Rebelling against obedience to God's law, Luther wrote to Melanchthon:

Sin, sin mightily, but have all the more confidence in Christ; rejoice more vehemently in Christ, who is the conqueror of sin, of death, and of the world. While we are in this world, we can do no other than sin; we must sin. This life is not the abode of righteousness; no, we merely await here, as St.

Peter says, "new heavens and a new earth, wherein dwelleth righteousness."

Pray earnestly, for thou art a great sinner.

I am now full of the doctrine of the remission of sins.

I grant nothing to the law, nor to all the devils. He who can believe in his heart this doctrine, is saved (Michelet 304).

Harboring a sense of guilt and condemnation anyway, Luther's mind evolved a doctrinal system whereby he could overthrow all law and the *rule* of God over our lives!

John Calvin was in much the same position. He had also grown up as a Catholic and was steeped in Catholic doctrines and concepts. Rebelling against the Roman church as a young man, he accepted Luther's arguments on salvation by faith *alone*.

But Calvin went one step further and developed his own theory of absolute *predestination*. As we have seen, this theory states: "For all men are not created on an equal footing, but *for some eternal life is preordained, for others eternal damnation*" (Bettenson 302).

We have already shown that this does violence to the frequent statement in the New Testament, "There is *no respect of persons with God*" (Romans 2:11; Acts 10:34; Ephesians 6:9, *KJV*). It also contradicts Paul's inspired description of "... God our Savior, who desires all men to be saved and to come to the knowledge of the truth" (1 Timothy 2:3–4). Is God's will to be thwarted by the reasonings of John Calvin?

And, of course, we must remember not only their actions, but also the false doctrines by which Calvin, Luther, and the English reformers tried to justify themselves for *imprisoning*, publicly *whipping*, *hanging*, *drowning*, or *burning alive* those who disagreed with their "pure" gospel teachings.

Rejecting or Distorting Scripture

At least in order to clear their own consciences, the Protestant leaders were forced to distort or reject many passages of Scripture which did not conform to their doctrinal ideas.

In defending his view of the "real presence" of the body and blood of Christ in the Eucharist, Luther argued that the *unbroken tradition* of the Roman Catholic Church ought to be proof in itself. Luther stated, "To deny such testimony is virtually to condemn not only the holy Christian church as a damned heretic, but even Christ himself, with all his apostles and prophets..." (Schaff 7: 531).

Schaff comments: "A Roman controversialist could not lay more stress on *tradition* than Luther does in this passage. But tradition, at least from the sixth to the sixteenth century, strongly favors the belief in transubstantiation, and the sacrifice of the mass, *both of which he rejected*" (Schaff 3: 532).

Thus, we see that Luther was *inconsistent*. When the Bible did not provide the answers he wanted, Luther looked to *Roman Catholic tradition!* But when this same tradition taught a doctrine or custom Luther disagreed with—such as transubstantiation—he turned with supposedly righteous indignation back to the Bible again.

In plain language, Luther was *self-contradictory* and *deceiving himself!*

He wanted to think he had the Bible on his side, yet whenever his unsound views of Scripture became apparent, he would run like a child to the arms of his "mother" church—and claim *Roman Catholic tradition* as his infallible guide.

Noted Protestant historians are forced to admit that Calvin and Zwingli as well as Luther distorted the plain meaning of Scripture to make it fit their own theories! "That principle Calvin took up and carried on; and as *Luther* found fault with the sacred writers whose utterances failed to fit in with his view of justification, so did *Zwingli*, and *Calvin even more consistently* than Zwingli, explain away all that seemed to limit or condition the truth on which they built" (Moore 389).

Again, commenting upon the tendency of the English theologians to follow Luther's interpretations of the Bible, Moore comments, "They cannot, therefore, shut their eyes to the fact that even Luther's devotion to the Bible was so tainted with *one-sidedness* that it contained in itself the seeds of decay" (Moore 479).

So, we find that the Protestant leaders often used *one-sided reasoning* to explain away any passage in the Bible that did not conform to their doctrines. They would reject such Catholic doctrines as transubstantiation and the selling of indulgences by appealing to the Bible. But when they did not agree with what *God* said in the Bible, they would resort to their own tainted *human reason* or appeal to the *tradition* of the *Roman Catholic Church*.

The Protestants Followed Rome

What is the meaning of this apparent hypocrisy? Was this the *"nothing but the Bible"*? Was this a restoration of the *true Church*? Here is the Protestants' own surprisingly candid admission!

Speaking of Luther, Fisher states, "In the retention of *rites* and *customs* he did not require an explicit authorization from Scripture. Enough that they were not forbidden, and are expedient and useful. His aversion to breaking loose from the essentials of *Latin Christianity* in matters of doctrine is equally manifest" (Fisher, *History of Christian Doctrine* 283). "The Reformers *inherited* the doctrine of persecution from their *mother Church...*" (Schaff 3: 700). Far more than most people even dream of, the Protestant leaders— *and the many churches springing from that movement*—have inherited *most* of their *doctrines*, their *concepts* of God and religion, and their *traditions* from the Roman Catholic Church—their original "mother" church.

Luther wished to retain many of the *rites* and *customs* of "Latin" or *Roman Catholic* practice, and many of their *doctrines* as well. In earlier portions of this thesis, we have seen how "some of the old *heathen feasts* became church festivals" (Hurlbut 79). We have noticed how the *pagan* festivals of Christmas and *New Year's* were adopted by the church in the *West—at Rome*—not by the original Church in and around Palestine (Fisher, *The History of the Christian Church* 119).

We remember Wharey's statement that by the close of the second century, "Christianity began already to wear the garb of *heathenism*" (Wharey 39). And we should consider again Plummer's comment: "And as soon as the revival of letters caused the contents of the New Testament and the teaching of the Fathers to be known, it was seen that what passed for Christianity at the close of the fifteenth century was *scarcely recognizable* as such, when placed side by side with what we know of Christianity at the close of the Apostolic Age" (Plummer 11).

The unanimous verdict of Protestant historians is that the Roman Catholic Church was *filled* with *paganism* and *iniquity*. Many of her *rituals* and *church festivals* were borrowed directly from the *pagan* religions and the ancient cult of sun worship.

Why is it, then, that the Protestants retained so many of the Roman Catholic *doctrines* and *rituals* and *religious festivals*? Why did they keep professing their *unity* with the paganized Roman system?

Part of the answer lies in the fact that they somehow felt that Rome was the *only* historical descendant of the true New Testament Church of God. Since, without recognizing their error, they were looking only for a big, organized denomination, and they felt that Rome *had* to be the only remnant of the true Church—in spite of her almost *total paganism.*

The Protestant historian D'Aubigne voices this common conception: "A mystery of iniquity oppressed the *enslaved* Church of Christ" (D'Aubigne 20). The reformers, having grown up from childhood as Roman Catholics, believed that this general religious system really constituted the true Church of God, but that somehow God had permitted it to become "enslaved" in a sink of iniquity.

Consequently, they felt that their task was to *purify* this foul system. Yet they sought to prove that they had not parted from the "essentials" of the Catholic system.

Luther said, "No one can deny that we hold, believe, sing, and confess all things in correspondence with the old Church, that *we make nothing new therein nor add anything thereto,* and in this way *we belong to the old Church and are one with it*" (Lindsay 1: 468).

By their *own* statements, then, it is *proved* that the Protestants regarded themselves only as a *continuation* of the historic *Catholic* church, but in a different and "purified" form. Luther himself vehemently affirms their essential *oneness* with the Catholic church!

Speaking of Calvin, Fisher tells us, "He did not deny that the Christian societies acknowledging the Pope are 'churches of Christ'... He indignantly denies that he has withdrawn from the Church" (Fisher, *History of Christian Doctrine* 304).

Schaff tells us that it is of the visible, or *historic Catholic church* that Calvin writes, "As our present design is to treat of the *visible Church,* we may learn even from her the title of *mother,* how useful and even necessary it is for us to know her" (Schaff 8: 450).

The insistence of the Protestant leaders on their *basic unity* with the Catholic church and their identification of her as their "mother" church is *most significant*!

God Identifies the Catholic Church

In the early editions of Martin Luther's translation of the New Testament, there are many illustrations picturing the "Whore of

Babylon" as the *Roman Catholic Church*. In describing this *widely understood interpretation*, Bainton tells us, "Fallen Babylon is plainly *Rome*" (Bainton 258).

Countless Protestant books, pamphlets, and tracts have made that same identification. They brand the Roman Catholic Church as the "great harlot" of Revelation 17.

But, it must be admitted, most of the more conservative Protestant denominational writers have stopped making this identification. After those first editions of the Bible, and early pamphlets and tracts, they suddenly came to the embarrassing realization that *they were telling on themselves*!

For in one of the most easily understood passages in this inspired prophetic book, God describes a great false religious system that was to arise, and labels it "Babylon the Great" (Revelation 17:1–6).

In a typical sense, the Bible clearly identifies a "woman" with a *church*. In 2 Corinthians 11:2 and in Ephesians 5:23, Paul describes the true Church as being in the position of a *wife*. Another example of this symbolism is the well-known prophecy concerning the *true* Church of God found in Revelation 12.

Remember that Jesus spoke of His Church as the "little flock." He taught that it was to be *scattered* and *persecuted* (Matthew 10:16–23; John 15:18–20). The Church of Revelation 12 is pictured as being *small* and *weak* of itself. It is pictured as a woman who must *flee into the wilderness* during the Middle Ages (Revelation 12:5–6). Certainly, this picture is exactly the *opposite* of the dominant, worldly, historical Roman Catholic Church!

This is the Church the reformers *should* have sought unity with, but did not. They *could not* because they *rejected* the *authority of God's law*! For the true Church is here pictured as a small remnant of believers "who *keep the commandments of God* and have the *testimony* of Jesus Christ" (v. 17).

In Revelation 19:7–9 the true Church is again pictured as a *woman*—the *bride* of Christ. She is arrayed in clean, white linen, which typifies "the *righteous acts* of the saints" (v. 8).

Returning to Revelation 17, we see that the woman pictured here is a fallen woman—a *"great harlot."* She sits upon "many waters." In verse 15, the prophecy itself identifies these waters as *"peoples, multitudes, nations, and tongues."*

This fallen church, then, is a *great* church—ruling over many nations and peoples. She is accused of having "committed fornication" with the kings of the earth. Spiritually, that could only mean that she is guilty of mixing in the *politics* and *wars* of this world.

Christ said that His kingdom is *not of this world* (John 18:36). James speaks of those who participate in the material lusts and wars of this world as spiritual *"adulterers"* (James 4:1–4).

The prophecy now becomes plain! This apostate church is condemned because she has played politics and participated in the politics and warfare of this world.

This fallen woman, or church, is arrayed in purple and scarlet colors. The purple symbolizes royal power and dignity. The scarlet signifies her spiritual whoredom!

She is a wealthy church "adorned with gold and precious stones and pearls" (Revelation 17:4). And, John writes, "I saw the woman, drunk with the blood of the saints and with the blood of the martyrs of Jesus. And when I saw her, I marveled with great amazement" (v. 6).

This church cruelly persecuted and martyred many of God's saints. But her wealth, her power, and her royal majesty inspired a sense of awe, even in John! Later, God reveals, "And the woman whom you saw is that great city which reigns over the kings of the earth" (v. 18).

The Prophecy Fulfilled

All of these descriptions apply *perfectly* to the *Roman Catholic Church! This* is the church that has persecuted God's scattered people down through the ages. This is the church which has had its own army and has been actively involved in the wars and politics of this world!

Only the capital of Catholic "Christendom" at Rome could truly be called a "great city" which has ruled over the kings of this world. *There is no mistaking this identification!*

Alexander Hislop, in his remarkable book, *The Two Babylons*, states, "There never has been any difficulty in the mind of any enlightened Protestant in identifying the woman 'sitting on seven mountains,' and having on her forehead the name written, 'Mystery, Babylon the Great,' with the Roman apostasy" (Hislop 1).

He tells us, "It has been known all along that Popery was baptized Paganism, but God is now making it manifest that the Paganism which Rome has baptized is, in all it's essential elements, *the very Paganism* which prevailed in the ancient literal Babylon, when Jehovah opened before Cyrus the two-leaved gates of brass, and cut in sunder the bars of iron" (Hislop 2).

In this most enlightening work, Hislop proceeds to *prove* that indeed the Roman Catholic Church adopted the *philosophies*, the *traditions*, and the *church festivals* of the ancient *pagans*. Roman Catholicism is nothing more than *baptized paganism!*

Hislop states that "Rome is in very deed the Babylon of the Apocalypse; that the essential character of her system, the grand object of her worship, her *festivals*, her *doctrine* and *disciplinc*, her *rites* and *ceremonies*, her *priesthood*, and their orders, have *all been derived from ancient Babylon*" (Hislop 3).

No wonder God calls this system "Mystery, Babylon the Great"! The Roman Catholic system contains the very *same doctrines*, *rituals* and *pagan religious holidays* as the ancient, heathen city of Babylon— so often used to typify *sin*.

But thus far we have left out *two important points*. The first is that in describing this *great false church*, John states that "the inhabitants of the earth were made *drunk* with the wine of her fornication" (Revelation 17:2). Hislop reveals that in the original Babylonian religion, the worshippers were *literally made drunk* so that they would favorably receive the pagan "mysteries" (Hislop 5).

This indicates that, as this entire chapter is speaking spiritually, the worshippers of Rome are made *spiritually drunk* so that they cannot see spiritual truths clearly. God says, "For all the nations have drunk of the wine of the wrath of her fornication" (Revelation 18:3).

These poisonous teachings and false concepts have crept into *every civilized nation on earth*. The peoples of the earth have become spiritually *drunk* on these false doctrines! When people then approach the Bible and the spiritual truths it contains, they become *mixed-up, confused* and *divided*.

"Babylon" literally means *confusion*. It is *great confusion*! It is "Babylon the Great"!

And doesn't this typify what we have seen of the Protestant reformers—arguing, bickering, divided even among themselves? And doesn't this describe the mixed-up, self-contradictory course taken by Luther, Calvin, and the other reformers?

The reformers were actually rebelling against only a *small part* of the Roman Catholic teachings. And they were as men *spiritually drunk*—not knowing where they wanted to go, or how to get there— still guided and misled by a background of *pagan* Roman doctrines and concepts. And, as we have seen, when they came out of the Roman Catholic Church they brought most of her teachings and traditions right along with them.

The Protestant Movement Identified

Now we should be able to understand clearly the full name and description of this whole apostate system!

It is given in Revelation 17:5: "And on her forehead a name was written: MYSTERY, BABYLON THE GREAT, THE MOTHER OF HARLOTS AND OF THE ABOMINATIONS OF THE EARTH."

The corrupt Roman "mother" church has given birth to *harlot daughters*! If the clear, consistent principles of Scriptural identification are to be honestly applied, the Protestant churches are "harlot daughters" of a paganized, apostate Rome!

They came *out of her* in protest. But, as we have clearly seen, they retained *most* of her pagan doctrines and concepts. They are still following Rome's example of mixing in the *politics* and *wars* of this world. And we have seen abundant *Protestant* testimony that they recognize her as their "mother" church!

One Protestant historian comments on Luther:

He started out to inaugurate a Church composed of those who had faith and spiritual vision, and who revealed an ability and power to proclaim the Word of God. But, in reality, he left in full operation a large relic of the *ancient creeds*, an extensive "rump" of *superstition, tradition*, and *magic*, and a heavy inheritance of external authority (Jones 228).

As Dr. Jones clearly implies, the Protestants still retain many pagan doctrines and traditions, which they inherited from Rome. We have observed that some of these false traditions involve the pagan holidays, which the early Catholics adopted and gave Christian-sounding names. We ought to *look into these things and understand them!*

The Protestant churches stand *clearly identified* by God Almighty as the *"harlot daughters"* of apostate Rome!

Speaking of this entire Babylonish system, God commands: *"Come out of her,* my people, lest you share in her sins, and lest you receive of her plagues"* (Revelation 18:4).

The question is whether or not we will *obey our Maker!*

The Real Meaning of the Reformation

In evaluating the *real meaning* of the Protestant Reformation, we must bear in mind *God's* purpose—not merely the purposes and standards of mortal men.

We are forced to conclude that the Reformation certainly did *not* lead men to "the Bible, the whole Bible, and nothing but the Bible" as Chillingworth would have us believe. And, even in essence, the Reformation did *not* return men to "the faith which was once for all delivered" (Jude 3).

Even on some of the side issues of public morality, the reformers were very grievously disappointed at the first fruits of their labors. "Such catastrophes as the Peasants' War and the monstrous behaviour of the wilder Anabaptists, to say nothing of the bitter controversies among the Protestants themselves, were disquieting enough, without adding to the account any deterioration, real or supposed, in the morality of private individuals" (Plummer 184).

In *spiritual drunkenness*, groping their way around apostate Rome, the reformers were not guided by the same *Spirit of God* that empowered the original apostles and *changed men's lives*. We must recognize that the leaders of the Reformation were only *transferring authority* to themselves *within* the same pagan system. Naturally, the spiritual "fruits" do not compare with inspired, original Christianity.

"To a large extent the true way of stating the case is not that the teaching of the Reformers had made men worse, but, that it had *failed to make them better*. And it is here that the parallel between the Reformation and the first preaching of the Gospel breaks down" (Plummer 189).

However, although they *completely failed* to restore the true religion of Jesus Christ, we may correctly say that Luther and the other reformers were used to accomplish at least two very worthwhile purposes. First, they freed men from the *binding authority* of the Catholic church, and the superstitious *fear* under which they were continually held (Plummer 136). And, secondly, misdirected as it sometimes was, they did give all men more real encouragement to *read the Bible for themselves.*

Even in the accomplishment of these two purposes, they were often aided by outside forces. The most potent of these were the *Renaissance*, which was already beginning to stir men to think for themselves even before the Reformation proper began, and the growth of *nationalism*, which was a powerful aid in breaking down any universal church authority.

We must acknowledge that in freeing men's minds from *some* error, the reformers added *much error* of their own devising. They did *not* turn men to the *truth*. Rather, they turned them to independent, *self-willed human reason.*

This has multiplied the already existing religious confusion. As we stated at the beginning of this book, the Protestant Reformation has spawned a veritable "Babylon" of religious denominations, sects, and religious movements.

This is *not* the "unity of the Spirit." This is *not* the one true Church Jesus Christ said He would build (Matthew 16:18).

Perhaps the only reason that Almighty God has allowed such confusion to exist in this age is so that the *true* Church of Revelation 12, Jesus' "little flock," may be permitted to carry the real *message* of Christ to the world just before He comes again.

For Jesus, the Son of God, said, "And this gospel of the kingdom will be preached in all the world as a witness to all the nations, and then the end will come" (Matthew 24:14).

Meanwhile, God tells us that we should *strive* to recapture "the faith which was once for all delivered." We should *live* "by every word of God."

And in His word, God describes this apostate, divided Catholic-Protestant religious system as "Babylon the Great." He commands us: "*Come out of her*" (Revelation 18:4).

God help you to *heed* what you have learned from this book! *Don't run from the **truth!*** The *end of this age* is near! "The time is fulfilled, and the kingdom of God is at hand. Repent, and believe in the gospel" (Mark 1:15).

The Reason Behind Today's Religious Confusion!

Human annihilation is far more possible than many believe! In a world torn by strife and hatred, man has now devised *several frightful ways* by which he can destroy all living things!

Year by year, this condition grows *worse*—not better! What is the *meaning* of these times?

In his first inaugural address, President Eisenhower solemnly stated:

> In the swift rush of great events, we find ourselves groping to know the full sense and meaning of the times in which we live.... How far have we come in man's long pilgrimage from darkness toward light? Are we nearing the light—a day of freedom and peace for all mankind? Or are the shadows of another night closing in upon us?... Science seems ready to confer upon us, as its final gift, *the power to erase human life from this planet.*

Yes, the **extinction** of all life is possible!

Unless God intervenes, we are headed for a time of *darkness* so much blacker than the Dark Ages that there can be no comparison!

Men do *not* know the way to bring *peace* to the world. We are living in a so-called "Christian" Western world. Yet it is a world *cut off from God,* groping in the dark, living under the constant threat of *world suicide!*

Why has our "Christianity" utterly **failed** to halt the mounting wave of *personal crime* among individuals—and international *gangsterism* among many of the world's leaders? *Why* do the organized church denominations have *no real answer* to these problems?

Has God Forsaken His People?

Fearful of the imminent use of *horrifying weapons* of mass destruction, many people are wondering: "Has God forsaken us?" The answer is that **we** *have forsaken God!* And we have forsaken Him *far more* than most of you even begin to realize.

Two thousand years ago, Jesus Christ came to this earth with a message from God the Father. He preached the good news of the kingdom—or government—of God (Mark 1:14). He also came to found His Church.

Jesus said, "I will build My church, and the gates of Hades shall not prevail against it" (Matthew 16:18).

Notice that Jesus did not say "churches" but *church*—**one** church. He called it the "little flock" (Luke 12:32).

Jesus taught His followers to *obey* God's spiritual law contained in the Ten Commandments. He said, "Whoever therefore breaks one of the least of these commandments, and teaches men so, shall be called least in the kingdom of heaven; but whoever does and teaches them, he shall be called great in the kingdom of heaven" (Matthew 5:19). Setting an example of perfect obedience to God's laws, Jesus told His disciples to become *perfect* in character, as is God Himself (Matthew 5:48).

Later, He warned His followers of ill treatment and persecution by the world, saying that "the time is coming that whoever kills you will think that he offers God service" (John 16:2).

But Jesus commanded His servants to continue preaching *His* message to the **end** of the age. Just before ascending to heaven, He commanded, "Go therefore and make disciples of all the nations, baptizing them in the name of the Father and of the Son and of the Holy Spirit, teaching them to observe all things that I have commanded you; and lo, I am with you always, even to the end of the age" (Matthew 28:19–20).

What most people completely fail to realize is that the true servants of God *were persecuted* and *were killed* down through the ages for preaching Christ's message! God's truth was *never* accepted by the world!

Jesus warned: "If they kept My word [they *crucified* Him instead!] they will keep yours also" (John 15:20).

Rather than *believing* and *obeying* Christ's message, this world has *persecuted* His servants and His true Church down to this day!

Early Apostasy

As we have seen and proved in this review of the Reformation, a startling *change* took place in nominal Christianity soon after the death of the original Apostles. *Paganism* was introduced into an apostate "Christianity," and God's **truth** was *suppressed* by clever argument and political pressure and, when necessary, by *physical force!*

We remember the historian Wharey's comment: "Christianity began already to wear the garb of heathenism" (Wharey 39). Hurlbut states, "The forms and ceremonies of *paganism* gradually crept into the worship. Some of the old *heathen feasts* became church festivals with change of name and worship" (Hurlbut 79).

You should realize that these *heathen practices* are *still being observed* by Catholic and Protestant Churches alike throughout the "Christian" world!

Describing the development of this paganized Roman Catholic system, the historian Hurlbut observes, "The church gradually usurped power over the state, and the result was not Christianity but a more or less corrupt *hierarchy* controlling the nations of Europe, making the church mainly a *political machine*" (Hurlbut 80).

Do you readers realize that in spite of these startling admissions by their own church historians, most Protestant ministers still attempt to prove their historical descent from Christ and His Apostles through the Roman Catholic Church? As we have seen before, they called her their "mother" church!

Yet, this apostate system *had departed* about as far from the teaching and practice of Jesus Christ and His Apostles as it would seem possible to imagine! The historian Plummer directly acknowledges this fact: "And as soon as the revival of letters caused the contents of the New Testament and the teaching of the fathers to be known, it was seen that what passed for Christianity at the close of the fifteenth century was *scarcely recognizable* as such, when placed side by side with what we know of Christianity at the close of the Apostolic Age" (Plummer 11).

Remember that Jesus said: "I will build My church." In Ephesians 1:22 and other scriptures, Christ is described as the *living* **Head** of the true Church. Do you imagine that He was the Head of this apostate, paganized system, which had utterly departed from almost every remnant of His true teaching and practice? Would He cause His faithful, commandment-keeping Church to descend through this foul system?

Failure of the Reformation

We have found in this book that the early Protestant reformers—and their later followers—completely *failed* to recapture the faith and practice of Jesus and His Apostles. We learned how both Calvin and Luther came at various points of truth from a background of Roman Catholic rearing, training, and education.

It seems that they found a few truths, only to introduce other peculiar errors of their own devising. And we found abundant historical records of how the early reformers *cruelly persecuted* those who disagreed with their teachings—even to the point of *taking their lives*!

Perhaps the most *basic reason* why these early reformers and their Protestant followers have not been able to understand the spiritual truths of the Bible and to believe and practice the literal teachings of Jesus is one *false concept* they have persistently maintained. They knew that Jesus said He would build His Church, and that it would not perish. Since they mistakenly felt that it would be a big, organized, *denominational body,* they immediately jumped to the conclusion that the Roman Catholic Church must be the connecting link between them and Jesus!

Therefore, much of their reasoning was based upon the early "traditions" and practices of that church—which they assumed to have been untainted by human reason. They continually looked to the "early fathers" of this church for guidance on doctrinal questions.

Remember that both Luther and Calvin were *reared* in Catholic homes, *trained* in Catholic schools, and *educated* for the Roman Catholic priesthood! They and their followers had grown up in a *Catholic* world. They were literally **saturated** with Catholic doctrines, concepts, and philosophies. As Almighty God shows in His word, they were spiritually *drunk* on the false doctrines of this paganized Catholic system!

No wonder they didn't embrace the "faith once for all delivered"! They looked to the example of the early Roman Catholic Church as to what that faith ought to be like. They could only see the present evils of the Catholic system in their own time. Little did they realize that the entire system was *completely* and *totally cut off from God,* from His Church, from His guidance!

Thus, these Protestant reformers and their later followers have *failed* to restore the *true message* of Jesus Christ to this earth! They have only introduced more religious confusion than already existed! So, God labels the whole system "Babylon the Great"—or *great confusion*!

Today's world, then, remains in almost total ignorance of Christ's real message—of the *purpose* of God, of the *laws* of God, of the *meaning* of the prophesied events being rapidly fulfilled at this very moment! But could this fantastic worldwide deception actually be possible? Could this be God's will?

A Counterfeit "Christianity" Prophesied!

Our modern religious *confusion* was prophesied hundreds of years ago in the Bible itself! Jesus Christ warned that *many* false preachers would come in His name—but would *deceive* the people by a false message. He said, "For *many* will come in My name, saying, 'I am the Christ,' and will *deceive* **many**" (Matthew 24:5).

Yes, *hundreds* of differing denominations have appropriated to themselves the *name* of Jesus Christ—but they have *denied* His message, and they have substituted *paganism* with its beliefs and practices for His way of life! And they have deceived the *many*—not the *few!*

The Apostle Paul was inspired to warn of this great departure from the Truth: "For the time will come when they will not endure sound doctrine, but according to their own desires, because they have itching ears, they will heap up for themselves teachers; and they will turn their ears away from the truth, and *be turned aside to fables*" (2 Timothy 4:3–4). Paul knew that after his death and that of the other apostles, false ministers *would* come in with all of their heathen practices, pagan religious festivals, and pagan philosophies. He knew that most would be turned from the truth to *fables—fairy tales!*

He warned of men in the last days "having a form of godliness but denying its power. And from such people turn away!" (2 Timothy 3:5). Paul knew that at the end of this age, men would cease to recognize God as a *power to be reckoned with* in world affairs—and that they would deny His *authority* in their individual lives.

The modern form of so-called Christianity is a *paganized* form! On the outside of the package it is labeled "Christianity." But *inside* are contained the old pagan philosophies, traditions, festivals and practices, and false concepts of God and the way of God.

Today's "Christianity" is *totally different* from the Christianity of Jesus Christ! Many recognized church historians admit this fact—seemingly oblivious of the tremendous *import* of what they are saying.

This Is a Deceived World!

A recognized and respected scholar, Dr. Rufus Jones, states: "If by any chance Christ Himself had been taken by His later followers as a model and a pattern of the new way, and a serious attempt had been made to set up His life and teaching as the standard and norm for the Church, Christianity would have been something *vastly different* from what it became" (Jones 16). Dr. Jones, a Protestant scholar, recognizes that the Christianity of Jesus is *not being practiced* in our modern world today!

Let us candidly inquire: What is *wrong* with **Jesus'** Christianity? Did Jesus Christ know what Christianity ought to be like? Just who *does* have the authority to set the standards for Christianity?

The real *answer* to this dilemma is that Christ Himself prophesied that the world would be *deceived* by Satan the devil and his false ministers. We find Satan described as "that serpent of old, called the Devil and Satan, who deceives the whole world" (Revelation 12:9). It seems hard to believe but the Bible says *this whole world has been deceived!*

Speaking of the Babylonish false religious system that developed during the Middle Ages, the Apostle John says in Revelation that "the inhabitants of the earth were made drunk with the wine of her fornication" (Revelation 17:2). Through the spiritual wine—or *false doctrines*—of this paganized system, the inhabitants of this *entire earth* have been made spiritually *drunk!*

Because of this spiritual confusion—this *spiritual drunkenness*—most people on earth today are not able to see spiritual things clearly. They are like a drunken man with blurry vision when they try to read the Bible. It doesn't make sense. They get confused. They may ask their minister—but usually only get an evasive answer or pretty platitude, which doesn't really answer the deep spiritual question in their heart.

The Bible just doesn't seem to make *sense* to people. They don't *understand* it. They don't understand the theme in its laws and teachings—and they certainly don't understand the *prophecies* of the Bible!

Satan's Counterfeit of the Truth

Almighty God has permitted Satan the devil to implant his religion in the minds of men here on earth. He began that clear back at the tower of Babel. He continued it through the ancient Chaldean mystery system developed by Nimrod and his harlot-wife, Semiramis. That system has spread over all the world, so that many of the *same customs* and *practices* of our so-called Western "Christianity" are found in varying forms throughout Asia and the pagan idolatry of the far-flung tropical islands!

This same Chaldean mystery system—with its pagan philosophies, its pagan religious holidays and symbols—was brought by stealth into many of the early Christian church congregations. Carnal-minded church leaders accepted this paganism, which the natural mind of man seems to love so much. They *pretended* it was Christianity—and incorporated it into an apostate Christianity they were beginning to develop out of those congregations and individuals who did not wish to keep intact the *way* and *truth* of God.

This pagan mystery system finally took over completely in the early Catholic church until it became, as we have seen, simply "baptized paganism." When the Protestant reformers were little children, they grew up as part of this system. They were taught it by their parents, friends, and teachers. They *believed* in it, and were even trained for its priesthood!

Both Luther and Calvin later *denied* that they had withdrawn from the historic Catholic church! This was because they felt that it *was* God's Church! Its basic *tenets* and *practices* they left *unchanged*. And even without their realizing it, the pagan philosophies and false concepts of God imparted by this system guided and influenced the development of Protestant religious teachings and outlook.

Now, in this age, *you* may have grown up supposing that all these churches are *God's* Churches. *You* have probably thought, "How can all these churches be wrong?"

They **can** be wrong, because God says, "For **all** the nations have drunk of the wine of the wrath of her fornication" (Revelation 18:3). Yes, *all* nations have been made spiritually drunk through Satan's deception coming down through the ancient Babylonish mystery system, into Roman Catholicism, and since to our modern Protestantism!

Truly, Satan *has* deceived "the whole world"! The Bible **means what it says** more than we have realized.

May God help you see this **truth!** You are not going to have long to debate about it, frankly, because we are nearing the *end* of this age of man going his own ways on earth.

Perhaps the absolutely real *threat of human annihilation* will force some of you to face spiritual *realities* in a way that you have never been willing to do before! God grant that it may be so before it is too late!

If you are willing to admit that you may have been *wrong*, then what should you do?

What You Should Do

First of all, you should review what was brought out about Christ and His Church in the first part of this work.

Jesus said, "I will build *My church*" (Matthew 16:18). He did not say *many* churches, but only indicated *one* Church—His Church! He called that Church the "little flock." He said they would be *scattered* and *persecuted*. Recall that in John 15:20, He said that the world would not keep to the truth of His Church, or accept it any more than they had accepted His own teachings directly from Him. Instead, they *crucified* Jesus Christ!

Remember that Jesus taught **obedience** to God's Law based on the Ten Commandments (Matthew 5:17–19; 19:17). He told His servants to continue preaching that same message. He commanded them to go into all nations, "teaching them to observe *all things* that *I have commanded you*" (Matthew 28:20).

In His revelation to John, Christ described the last-generation remnant of His Church as those people "who keep the commandments of God and have the testimony of Jesus Christ" (Revelation 12:17). He describes His persecuted saints as follows: "Here is the patience of the saints; here are those who keep the **commandments** of God and the faith of Jesus" (Revelation 14:12).

If you want to know the *truth*, if you want to be protected from the hellish times of world cataclysm that lie just ahead, then *you had better seek for and find that Church!* You had better find the true Church of God—the only Church Jesus built—the Church of which He is the living Head!

Has there been a small, scattered, persecuted Church which keeps *all* of God's Commandments and which Jesus Christ is using as His "body" today in doing His Work in preaching His Gospel to the world?

Yes! There *has been* and *is*. But first you need to *prove* this—and then you need to *do something about it!*

Proofs of God's Church

All of the scriptures already mentioned should apply to God's true Church—*not just part of them*. And God's Church will be keeping *all ten* of the Ten Commandments contained in God's spiritual law. You need to be especially sure of this point and *study* your Bible to find out more about God's law, yourself! For as we have seen, the true Church is commonly identified as that people "who keep the *commandments* of God."

Another thing to bear in mind in regard to the true Church being scattered and persecuted is that you can't "join" that Church like you would some social club! In New Testament times, people were only considered members of God's Church after they had obeyed the inspired command, "**Repent,** and let every one of you **be baptized in the name of Jesus Christ for the remission of sins**; and you shall **receive the gift of the Holy Spirit**" (Acts 2:38). So, you have to *repent* of your sins and of your entire rebellious, self-willed way of life before God will put you into His Church!

After repentance and baptism, you are to practice—as we have seen—*obedience* to God's law as a way of life. You are to live by *every word of God* and to follow the literal example and teaching of Jesus Christ.

Another outstanding characteristic of God's Church is its willingness to *admit error* and to *change*. Each human is commanded to *change*—to *grow in grace and in knowledge* (2 Peter 3:18). Since the Church is only the sum total of its members, it, too, must continually be willing to repent if there is some minor error God has permitted to creep in, and to *grow* in grace and in knowledge.

Therefore, the true Church will be a body of people continually *growing* into more complete truth and knowledge and deeper understanding! Its members will "hunger and thirst" for righteousness (Matthew 5:6). Because of this humble, repentant, yielded attitude, it will be *filled* with love and zeal and a continually deeper **understanding** of God's will and of the meaning of Bible prophecies in relation to the times in which we live.

These things are so because God's Church is yielded to and led by His Spirit! And Jesus said it is the *Spirit* that leads us into all truth (John 16:13). *Only* God's true Church really has these characteristics! And therefore, *only* God's true Church is filled with the *knowledge*, the *understanding*, and the *love* of His Spirit!

The Name of God's Church

In addition to being a small persecuted Church kept completely separate from the pagan doctrines, religious holidays, and heathen philosophies fostered by "mother" Rome, and in addition also to the fact that it keeps *all ten* of the Ten Commandments of God, and that it has the right spiritual attitude and willingness to repent, to change, to grow—the true Church should also have the *name* God intended His Church to bear as one of its identifying signs.

God's true Church was *never* named after some religious leader, or some particular doctrine, or some type of church government or method of doing things! Scripture shows that it was *always* named after God Himself! It is *His* Church. He owns it. He possesses it. He *rules it*—through His Son Jesus Christ who is also God (John 1:1). Therefore, in *twelve places* in the New Testament it is called the "Church of God."

In Acts 20:28, Paul told the Ephesian elders to shepherd "the church of God" as he was speaking to them, perhaps for the last time. Both of the letters to the Corinthian Church are addressed to "the church of God which is at Corinth."

Speaking of the Church congregations collectively, Paul writes to the Thessalonians, "For you, brethren, became imitators of the churches of God which are in Judea in Christ Jesus" (1 Thessalonians 2:14).

In *every case* when the title is given in any official sense, the name for the Church is "the Church of God." That is the *inspired* **name** of God's Church!

However, since most churches have at least a few points of truth, some of them have *falsely* appropriated to themselves the name "Church of God." But they are *not* His Church because they do not keep His commandments, do not have His Spirit, and are not doing His *Work*.

Find Out Where God Is Working

Just as important as having the correct *name* and possessing the other characteristics we have discussed, the true Church must be doing the *Work of God* on earth today!

It must be preaching Christ's true *message,* His *command-ments,* His *way of life*. It must be preparing the way for God's Kingdom—or government—to come and rule this earth before man destroys himself.

God's true Church is the one which will be *warning* the peoples and nations of the world of specific *punishments*, which Almighty God is *already* beginning to mete out. God's true Church, then, will really *understand* and *proclaim* the warning messages contained in Bible prophecy, as God's *witness* to a rebellious world!

Do *you* know where to find that Church?

You are *now reading* one of the warning messages from the true Church of God —the *body* of Christ—the *instrument* God is using to preach His message! If you do not already know, the day will come when you *will* know that *this is the Work of God's true Church!*

The message now being proclaimed *around this earth* by the *Tomorrow's World* telecast, magazine, and website is the Work of the Church Jesus Christ built—and of which He is the living, executive Head!

For decades, this Church has dared, *as no other church on earth*, to proclaim definite, specific prophetic events to occur—and *they have been happening!*

So that some may *repent* and be spared, God is using this Church to *warn* the peoples of this world of their mounting *sins* before He intervenes to *punish* through the plagues and hardships to come just prior to Christ's second coming. God help *you* to understand and to heed this warning!

Have you noticed that this book, along with the *Tomorrow's World* telecast and magazines, are both sponsored by the *Living Church of God?*

That is because *this* Church is *God's* Church! He is using it to do *His* Work, and so it carries *His* name!

Take Heed to the Truth!

The warning message of God's Church is being fulfilled *daily!*

Scoffers will not have long to scoff! For the *specific* prophesied events, which this Church proclaims, will increasingly be demonstrated as physical *reality!* There will be no reasoning or argument about this. You will *see* and *feel* these things happen!

The reason God has allowed today's religious confusion is so that after 6,000 years of human misrule—bringing us now to the verge of *world suicide*—man might at last "have enough" of his *own* ways, his *own* political schemes, his *own* religious theories.

After a time of *great punishment* which he has brought on himself, man will at last be really *willing* to learn of *God's* ways and laws, and to accept *His* rule through Jesus Christ so the world can at last have *peace!*

God has *permitted* this "Babylon" of religious confusion to develop so that man might be able—under Satan's deceiving influence—to try out every conceivable type of religious theory he might lust after.

This is so that man might—in plain language—once and for all get his "belly full" of the foolish ideas and reasoning of *carnal*, human, erring *men*. Then, perhaps, he will be willing to *obey God!*

Now you know *why* there exists such religious confusion. Now you know which is the *true* Church of God!

This is **your** *life!*

May the Almighty give you an open mind to further *prove* and *believe* His *truth!* That *truth* is given in abundance in every issue of the *Tomorrow's World* magazine. Study our resources. Look up the scripture references in *your own Bible.*

Watch the *Tomorrow's World* telecast regularly, and check out all we make available on our website in the same way: *with your Bible open.* Write for and read *every booklet* that is mentioned. They are all *free!*

Pray for understanding and for a *willing heart!* Be sure to obey the truth as you prove each point.

This is the most important business of your life! The *end* of this age is *very near!*

Works Cited

Alzog, John. *Manual of Church History*. Dublin: Warner, 1996.

Babington, J. A. *The Reformation*. London: John Murray, 1901.

Bainton, Roland H. *Here I Stand*. New York: The New American Library, 1956.

Bainton, Roland H. *The Reformation of the Sixteenth Century*. London: Hodder and Stoughton Ltd., 1953.

Bettenson, Henry. *Documents of the Christian Church*. New York: Oxford University Press, 1947.

D'Aubigne, J. H. Merle. *History of the Reformation*. London: Religious Tract Society, 1846.

Deharbe, Joseph. *A History of Religion*. London: Burns and Cates, 1881.

Fisher, George P. *History of Christian Doctrine*. Edinburgh: T. & T. Clark, 1896.

Fisher, George P. *History of the Christian Church*. New York: Charles Scribner's Sons, 1897.

Fisher, George P. *The Reformation*. New York: Scribner, Armstrong, and Co., 1873.

Gibbon, Edward. *The Decline and Fall of the Roman Empire*. New York: Siegel-Cooper Co., 1845.

Hastie, William. *The Theology of the Reformed Church in its Fundamental Principles*. Edinburgh: T. & T. Clark, 1904.

Hausser, Ludwig. *The Period of the Reformation*. London: J. S. Virtue & Co., Ltd., 1885.

Herzog, J. J., Schaff, Philip. *Schaff-Herzog's New Encyclopedia of Religious Knowledge*. New York: Funk and Wagnalls Co., 1910.

Hislop, Alexander. *The Two Babylons*. New York: Loizeaux Brothers, 1948.

Hurlbut, Jesse Lyman. *The Story of the Christian Church*. Philadelphia: The John C. Winston Co., 1933.

Jones, Rufus M. *The Church's Debt to Heretics*. London: James Clarke & Co., Ltd., 1924.

Kurtz, J.H. *Church History*. London: Hodder and Stoughton, 1889.

Lindsay, Thomas M. *A History of the Reformation*. Edinburgh: T. & T. Clark, 1907.

MacKinnon, James. *Calvin and the Reformation*. London: Longmans, Green, and Co., 1936.

Michelet, M. *The Life of Luther*. London: David Bogue, Fleet Street, 1846.

Moncrief, John W. *A Short History of the Christian Church*. New York: Fleming H. Revell Co., 1902.

Moore, Aubrey Lackington. *Lectures and Papers on the History of the Reformation*. London: Kegan Paul, Trench, Trübner & Co., Ltd., 1890.

Works Cited

Mosheim, John Laurence. *Institutes of Ecclesiastical History*. London: Ward, Lock, & Co., 1847.

Neander, Augustus. *General History of the Christian Religion and Church*. London: Henry G. Bohn, 1858.

Perrin, Jean Paul. *History of the Old Waldenses, Anterior to the Reformation*. New York: P. Miller, 1884.

Plummer, Alfred. *The Continental Reformation*. London: Robert Scott, 1912.

Qualben, Lars P. *A History of the Christian Church*. New York: Thomas Nelson and Sons, 1942.

Schaff, Philip. *History of the Christian Church*. Grand Rapids: Wm. B. Eerdman's Publishing Co., 1950.

Vedder, Henry C. *A Short History of the Baptists*. Philadelphia: The American Baptist Society, 1907.

Walker, Reginald F. *An Outline of the Catholic Church*. Dublin: M. H. Gill and Son, Ltd., 1950.

Walker, Williston. *A History of the Christian Church*. New York: Charles Scribner's Sons, 1949.

Wharey, James. *Sketches of Church History*. Philadelphia: Presbyterian Board of Publication, 1840.

Regional Offices

United States
PO Box 3810
Charlotte, NC 28227-8010
Phone: +1 (704) 844-1970

Australasia
PO Box 300
Clarendon, SA 5157, Australia
Phone: +61 8 8383 6266

Canada
PO Box 409
Mississauga, ON L5M 0P6
Phone: +1 (905) 814-1094

New Zealand
PO Box 2767
Shortland Street
Auckland 1140
Phone: +64 9-268 8985

Philippines
PO Box 492
Araneta Center Post Office
1135 Quezon City, Metro Manila
Phone: +63 2 8573 7594

South Africa
Private Bag X3016
Harrismith, FS 9880
Phone: +27 58 622 1424

United Kingdom
Box 111
88-90 Hatton Garden
London EC1N 8PG
Phone/Fax: +44 844 800 9322